The LOST PATROL

The LOST PATROL

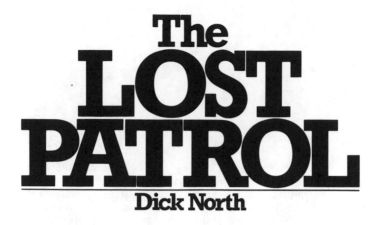

Dick North

ALASKA NORTHWEST PUBLISHING COMPANY
Anchorage, Alaska

Fifth printing 1987

Library of Congress cataloging in publication data:
North, Dick
    The lost patrol.
    Bibliography: p.
    1. Northwest Territories—History.   2. Canada.
Royal Canadian Mounted Police.   I.   Title.
F1060.9.N65   971.9'1   78-1368
ISBN 0-88240-106-8

Design & CartoGraphics by Jon.Hersh

Alaska Northwest Publishing Company
Box 4-EEE, Anchorage, Alaska 99509
Printed in U.S.A.

Dedicated to
Charley Rivers, Richard Martin,
Andrew Kunnizzi, Charles Thornback,
Frank Fitzgerald, Jack Dempster
and to all of the men who made the Dawson City-
Fort McPherson Patrol.

Contents

Acknowledgments ix

Introduction 1

Chapter 1
Herschel Island 6

Chapter 2
Klondike Patrol: Edmonton to Fort Grahame 10

Chapter 3
Klondike Patrol: Fort Grahame to the Yukon 24

Chapter 4
Fitzgerald at Herschel Island 30

Chapter 5
The Route to Fort McPherson 42

Chapter 6
Early Patrols 50

Chapter 7
Life on the Trail 58

Chapter 8
The Fatal Patrol 88

Chapter 9
Death on the Trail 100

Chapter 10
Reflections 116

Epilogue 126

Appendices 132
Bibliography 136

Acknowledgments

Many people, too numerous to mention, generously and unstintingly gave me their help and support during the long months of research and writing of this book. I am forever indebted to them all. A few, however, must be singled out for their particular contributions.

Grateful thanks, therefore, go to George Robertson, writer of the script and lead actor for the CBC television production, "The Dawson Patrol," who contributed valuable information concerning Inspector Fitzgerald's life at Herschel Island and operations from Fort McPherson; Margaret Carter and the staff of the National Archives in Ottawa, who guided me through the labyrinth and helped unearth old patrol reports; Stan Horrall of the historical section of the Royal Canadian Mounted Police, who never failed to answer queries sent his way; Annette Lucier of the Yukon Territorial Library, who added important facts about Frank Fitzgerald's participation in the pioneering Klondike patrol; Charles Thornback, Andrew Kunnizzi, Richard Martin and Charley River, each of whom made the Dawson City-Fort McPherson patrol, for personally reliving for me the way the way of life on the trail of the early patrols; Bob De Armond, past editor of "The Alaska Journal," who uncovered little-known facts about Herschel Island; Joe and Annie Henry, who described life in the upper Peel River region, and who introduced me to former guide Richard Martin; the late Mother Superior Sara Fitzgerald of Taipei, Formosa, who shed light on F. J. Fitzgerald's days at home in Nova Scotia, and Ida Spearns, who contributed information about his youth; Ida (Ninagaserk) Bennett for her description of life on the Arctic Coast; Major Frank Riddell, Royal Canadian Signals, Retired, veteran Arctic traveler and expert on survival, for his comments on the rations and operating procedures of the Fitzgerald patrol; dietitian Winston Osborn, who provided expert analysis of the nutritional value of the rations Fitzgerald carried; explorer Amos Burg, who supplied photos and provided guidance in writing the book; Barbara Kinneen, who provided valuable criticism of the manuscript; Becky Vandermeer and Carol Elliott for their typing; and to editor Edward Day, whose discerning eye was indispensable to the completion of the book.

Finally, this book would never have been started were it not for Tom Coleman, former RCMP corporal who knew many of the men who made the 950-mile patrol and who himself made many dog-team patrols in the Yukon. It was he who originally incited my interest in the Fitzgerald tragedy.

"I demand that neither hardship, suffering, privation, nor fear of death should move you by a hair's breadth from carrying out your duties."

Inspector George French
Royal North-West Mounted Police

Introduction

On February 27, 1911, Corporal W.J.D. Dempster of the Royal North-West Mounted Police received the following ominous message from Superintendent A. E. Snyder, in command of B Division of the Mounties:

You will leave tomorrow morning for a patrol over the Fort McPherson trail, to locate the whereabouts of Inspector Fitzgerald's party. Indians from McPherson reported him on New Year's Day at Mountain Creek. Fair travelling from Mountain Creek [is] about 20 days to Dawson. I understand that at Hart River Divide no matter what route he took, he would have to cross this divide. I think it would be advisable to make for this point and take up his trail from there. I cannot give you any specific instructions; you will have to be guided by circumstances and your own judgment, bearing in mind that nothing is to stand in your way until you have got in touch with this party.

Dempster was then in Dawson City, Yukon Territory, having been summoned there from his regular post at Forty Mile on February 20. He assembled his patrol and set out on February 28. But by the date of Snyder's order, Inspector Francis Joseph Fitzgerald and the three men of his patrol, Constable George Frances Kinney, Constable Richard O'Hara Taylor and ex-Constable Samuel Carter, had already died from hunger, exposure and exhaustion. They had died less than 35 miles from their starting point at Fort McPherson, Northwest Territories, after spending 53 days and traveling 620 miles on the trail. Lesser men would have quit much sooner.

The Lost Patrol of the Mounted Police perished while

1

traversing the deep wilderness between Fort McPherson and Dawson City. It was a routine, annual patrol that had been inaugurated in the winter of 1904-5. After the loss, Commissioner A. Bowen Perry of the Mounties termed it "the greatest tragedy which has occurred in this Force during its existence of 37 years."

The epic battle of the four Mounties to stay alive when hope was all but gone has become a fixture in Northern lore. Seldom can people gather around a campfire or get together in the convivial atmosphere of a Northern tavern without the subject of the Lost Patrol coming up. Men speculate on the reasons for the failure of the patrol of 1910-11, and almost everyone has an opinion on how *he* would have avoided disaster. The Mounties of that period traveled tens of thousands of miles every year by dog team throughout northern Canada. The wonder is that it took 37 years before a tragedy such as that of the Lost Patrol occurred. The Dawson-McPherson patrol entails all of the romance, legend and mystery that comprise the lore of the Arctic and sub-Arctic. In a sense, it is where legend and reality become one.

The region where Fitzgerald and his men were lost encompasses numerous mountain ranges and the drainage of the Peel River. Six major rivers contribute to the Peel River drainage: the Ogilvie, Blackstone, Hart, Wind, Bonnet Plume and the Snake. Even today, only two of these rivers are touched by a road, the Dempster Highway, named after Inspector Dempster who commanded the Mountie patrol that found the bodies of the four lost men.

At the time of writing, the Dempster Highway was still under construction. It reached the Blackstone River in the early 1960s, then was halted. The project was begun again in 1970. At this time, I was fisheries warden for the northern district of the Yukon Territory, which includes the Blackstone River and the Dempster Highway. If one drives up the highway, he will see a sign at Mile 78 marking the point where the road crosses the old Mountie dog-sled trail. Shortly before the driver reaches this point, if it is spring, he will see a tent camp surrounded by racks of caribou skins, and if he is lucky, he will see Annie and Joe Henry. They are the last residents (and only for part of the year) of Black City, which was a stopover point for the Mountie patrols on their way from Dawson City to Fort McPherson. Black City (short for Blackstone City) was a Loucheux Indian camp that once numbered 50 to 60 people. Over 70 years ago, Annie Henry was born there. Joe was born farther north, on the fringe of the Richardson Mountains, but for years trapped and hunted in the territory through which the Mounties passed.

Joe's uncles, John and Richard Martin, guided the Mountie patrols. A cousin of Joe's, Andrew Kunnizzi, served as both trailbreaker and guide on two of the Dawson-McPherson patrols. During one of my visits with Joe and Annie at their permanent home in Dawson, they took me to visit Richard, and it was my good fortune to hear Richard's impression of guiding the first patrol of 1904-5, led by Constable Harry G. Mapley, and the third patrol, which had been led by Constable A. E. Forrest in 1906-7. Richard said the patrols had been a rugged experience, and he had had no desire to join more of them. His brother John took the job in 1907-8, and then on and off until the patrols were stopped in 1921.

Richard Martin (who died during the winter of 1974-5 at the age of 95) was a very capable man in the bush, so for him to say that the 475-mile patrol was difficult means that it would be well-nigh impossible for the average man to complete today. This assessment is reinforced by Charley Rivers, who made the trip once and was not ready to make it a second time. Charley was acknowledged to be a fine hunter and woodsman.

It *was* tough. The men who made the patrol have ever since been held in high esteem by fellow members of the Royal Canadian Mounted Police.

In order to fully comprehend what occurred during the patrol of 1910-11, we need to examine not only the details of the patrol itself, but the history of the coming of the Mounties to the region, and most of all, the career of the leader of the Lost Patrol, Inspector Francis J. Fitzgerald.

Fitzgerald's place in the history of the North has largely

3

been ignored, or if not ignored, has suffered from a tendency to cast him as a martinet who, like Custer, led his men to a tragic death. Fitzgerald deserves better than this. His accomplishments in so short a life span—41 years—were considerable. At 27 he was one of the pioneer surveyors of an all-Canadian overland route from Edmonton to the Klondike on the famous Mountie patrol headed by Inspector J. D. Moodie. When he was 29 he fought in the Boer War, and he commanded the first Mountie detachment on the Arctic Ocean at 34. Fitzgerald was 36 when he completed a dog-sled patrol from Dawson City to Herschel Island in the Beaufort Sea, making him one of but a handful of men who could claim to have traveled overland from Edmonton to the Arctic coast by way of Interior British Columbia and the Yukon Territory. He was promoted to inspector when he was 40 years old.

According to a dispatch dated April 18, 1911, Lieutenant Colonel White, comptroller of the Royal North-West Mounted Police, was quoted as saying in Ottawa that Inspector Fitzgerald and the three men with him—Carter, Kinney and Taylor—were to be selected for the Mountie contingent to the coronation of King George V. No greater honor could have been bestowed on any of its members by an appreciative organization. However, fate had other things in store for Fitzgerald and his men.

This is their story.

Chapter 1
Herschel Island

The arrival of American whaling ships at Herschel Island in the Arctic Ocean in 1889 was to set in motion a sequence of events that would bring Francis Fitzgerald to the island in 1903, and ultimately lead to his death while commanding the Lost Patrol 8 years later.

On August 11, 1889, one year after Fitzgerald joined the North-West Mounted Police, the first whaling ships, all of American registry, ventured around Point Barrow eastward into Canadian Arctic waters. The ships were the *Lucretia, Jessie Freeman, Orca, Narwhal, Thrasher, William Lewis* and *Grampus.* They anchored off the east side of Herschel Island, a small, barren, windswept landmass 8¼ miles long and 4½ miles wide, about 15 miles off the coast of the Yukon Territory and 50 miles from the border of Alaska. Herschel, 180 miles north of the Arctic Circle, was first surveyed in 1889 by Commodore Stockton of the U.S. Navy, aboard the Revenue Cutter *Thetis.*

Several of the whalers ventured as far east as the Mackenzie River. However, the *Jessie Freeman* found a shoal at less than 4 fathoms, 15 miles off land near Herschel Island, and her report promptly scared most of the ships into retreating westward, the way they had come.

Two of the ships, less timid than the others, remained in the area 10 days, and each caught two bowhead whales. These ships, the *Orca* and *Thrasher,* were the first to catch whales off Herschel Island. They, too, then headed west in a hasty retreat to avoid becoming ensnared in the arctic ice pack. But the idea of spending a winter in the Arctic in order to gain the advantage of an entire ice-free season on the whaling grounds had taken hold. The captains and crewmen of the ships real-

6

ized that if they came North sufficiently equipped to spend a winter, they could increase their profits enormously by eliminating the time-wasting round trip to San Francisco.

The next year the *Grampus* and *Mary D. Hume* arrived at Herschel Island with enough provisions to last for 2 years. They sounded out a channel and found an anchorage in Pauline Cove, a small bay 700 yards long and 600 yards wide. The cove, with 3 fathoms of water, was deep enough for many ships to winter over in comparative safety, despite frequent gales. By mid September of 1890, the two ships were frozen in.

The men of the whaling ships were practical in every way, and soon had a comfortable camp set up. They purchased caribou meat from the local Eskimos, whom they called *Itkillicks*, sawed ice for fresh water from a pond on the island and melted it in a special stove equipped with a water tank, and even built sheds over the superstructure of the ships with lumber brought along for the purpose.

A woman struggling with her corset in the more civilized parts of the world probably knew that it was braced with whalebone stays, but it is not likely she realized the lengths to which men had to go to catch the whales that supplied the bone. As early as the 1840s, whalers were harpooning bowhead whales in the Bering Sea off the coast of Alaska. The industry had to be worth the effort, and it was.

There are 780 slabs of bone in the mouth of a bowhead whale, or about a ton of bone per mature animal. The going rate for this bone in the 1890s was $5 per pound, which meant that each whale was worth about $10,000 for its bone alone. The *Orca* and *Thrasher* each had made $20,000 in the 10 days they were off Herschel Island in 1889. During the period from 1889 to 1906, an estimated 1,345 whales were taken in Canadian waters. The harvesting of this resource, along with occasional trading for furs, brought the whalers approximately $15 million. The Canadian government soon became aware that most of the whalers, who were realizing substantial profits from this "Canadian" product, were not citizens, yet were using a Canadian harbor as a base for their operations.

The local Eskimos wasted no time in setting up trade with the newcomers. Caribou meat and skins were bartered for rifles, powder, cartridges and calico. Illegal to begin with, the trading took a turn for the worse when liquor entered the picture. It did not take the sea captains long to realize the native weakness for alcohol, and this soon began to take the place of bona-fide trade goods. Furs and women were introduced into the trade for booze. Reports of unruly behavior made their way back to Ottawa, where they were referred to the North-West Mounted Police. These reports were ultimately confirmed when an Anglican missionary, the Reverend C. E. Whittaker, wrote a lengthy note to the Canadian government to complain of the bitter treatment the Natives were getting at the hands of the whalers. The missionary contended that the debauch at Herschel Island was unparalleled in the history of the Arctic. (Whittaker's predecessor, Reverend I. O. Stringer, had made earlier protestations to the whaling captains with little success.)

Thus, there were three good reasons for Canada to formally establish her presence in the region: to collect duty on whales taken from her territorial jurisdiction; to stop the illegal trading; to calm the ruffled waters on a "sea of sin." And there was another good reason—to establish sovereignty over the area. The Mounties had done this in 1874 when they marched west to establish jurisdiction in the prairies, and later when they sent their red-coated representatives into the Yukon shortly before the gold rush of 1897-8.

To accomplish this at Herschel Island, a Mountie detachment would have to be sent to the Arctic and a string of posts established. It was decided to establish two posts, one at Herschel Island, and one at Fort McPherson, on the right bank of the Peel River, 30 miles above its junction with the Mackenzie River. A staff sergeant would be named to command the detachment, which was responsible for the two posts. This man would have to be an individual capable of independent thought and action. He would have to be a man of impeccable honesty and tenacious will. He would have to be able to stand the solitude of the Arctic coast, yet remain incorruptible. He would have to know how to mush a dog team, and have years of experience on the trail. Above all, he would have to be a man of intelligence whom the Mounties knew they could depend upon in any situation.

The man they chose was a veteran of 15 years service, Sergeant Francis J. Fitzgerald, who was sent to Herschel Island in the summer of 1903. Fitzgerald had already had enough adventure to last the average man three lifetimes, and since the story of the Lost Patrol is also the story of its leader, it seems proper to review his first 15 years with the Royal North-West Mounted Police.

Chapter 2
Klondike Patrol: Edmonton to Fort Grahame

Frank Fitzgerald enlisted in the North-West Mounted Police on November 19, 1888, after quitting his job as a shoe salesman in Halifax, Nova Scotia. Later, the Mounties had some difficulty determining his real age, as he had added several years at the time of his enlistment. He was born on April 12, 1869, the son of a Western Union employee. He lived in Halifax up to the time of his enlistment and returned only rarely afterwards.

Records show that the lad had no trouble passing the Mountie physical, though at that time he was slight of build. (Reports in later years characterize him as a man of rugged build—the result of many years on the trail.) He was listed as an average recruit with good intelligence.

Fitzgerald reported to the recruit school in Regina, Saskatchewan. After completing the course, he went on to serve for the next few years with but one blemish on his record, which occurred soon after he graduated and was the result of a losing bout with a bottle of overproof rum. A corporal remonstrated with the rookie, and Fitzgerald rashly told the NCO to go jump in the lake (or perhaps to go to a less pleasant place). Fitzgerald was called on the carpet for a short lecture by Commissioner Herchmer, who warned the youngster that any further mischief would result in his being dismissed from the Force.

Fitzgerald served for the next 9 years with exemplary conduct at Fort Saskatchewan, Wetaskiwin and Maple Creek. Either he refrained from drinking overproof rum, or he learned how to handle it better.

Then came the year 1897. Gold had been discovered in the Klondike in 1896 and the word flashed around the world. The great Hegira to the Klondike began. Tens of thousands of people headed toward the northwest corner of what was then the Yukon District of the Northwest Territories of Canada. The shortest route was up the west coast by ship, then across the coast range to the headwaters of the Yukon River, and down the river to Dawson City. Dawson was the supply point for the Klondike strike a few miles away on Bonanza Creek. The cities benefitting from this route were the coastal towns of Seattle and Vancouver. Edmonton attempted to divert the tide rushing through those cities by advertising itself as a jump-off point for an all-Canadian route to the Klondike.

Hordes of stampeders started out, route or no, and hundreds of them became scattered over the country from Edmonton, north. The situation grew so bad during the summer of 1897 that the Mounties were asked to survey a route from Edmonton to the Yukon River. As a rule, the Mounties were not supposed to be surveyors or road builders, but they were probably asked to do this job because the government felt the policemen could settle any disputes they found along the way, utilizing their law enforcement capability along with that of exploration. Inspector J. D. Moodie was ordered to lead the expedition.

About 1,200 miles of virtually uncharted sub-arctic wilderness lay between Edmonton and the Yukon District. Moodie was stationed at Maple Creek, Saskatchewan, at the time of his assignment to the Northern trek. Four other men received orders to accompany him on his historic journey: F. J. Fitzgerald, Richard Hardisty, and two graduates from the Royal Military College, Frank Lafferty and H. S. Tobin.

In addition, Baptiste Pepin, a metis, was hired to run the packstring of 31 horses.

Commissioner L. W. Herchmer told Moodie what results he expected from the expedition. They were considerable. He wanted a map drawn showing the best route from Edmonton to the headwaters of the Pelly River, a tributary of the Yukon, the portions of the trail over which wagons could be driven at the least expense, the parts of the trail needing grading and ditching and favorable sites for grazing animals. He also wanted reports on all rivers and creeks that needed ferries or bridges, and the potential for hunting game animals along the route. Commissioner Herchmer added that Inspector Moodie, on completion of his journey, should be able to supply enough reliable information to advise a party leaving Edmonton of everything it could expect at all points along the way.

The route Herchmer suggested Moodie follow was from Edmonton to the Peace River, and along that river to Fort St. John. From Fort St. John they were to cross the Rockies to the Finlay River and to follow that north along the Rocky Mountains to Fort Grahame. Their route from that point went over Sifton Pass and eased northwest until they reached Deadwood Lake and Sylvester Landing, on the Dease River. From there, Herchmer advised Moodie to take whatever route he wanted to reach the Pelly River. In fact, Herchmer gave options to Moodie over most of the route, but there was no option concerning getting there—that was an order.

The experience Frank Fitzgerald was to acquire on this expedition would place him among the ranks of veteran trailsmen who were accorded the highest respect by other members of that famous police force. The Moodie patrol ran into every conceivable problem associated with a Northern trek.

September 4, 1897, while thousands of men were struggling up Chilkoot Pass on the Alaskan approach to the Klondike, Frank Fitzgerald and his companions set out from Edmonton on the first leg of the pioneering trek. They literally chopped, hacked, slashed and swam their way from Edmonton to Fort St. John.

Their trail followed the course that Route 43 runs today. Almost every day of the first leg of the trip was an agonizing battle with the elements, and if the elements occasionally relaxed their harassment, the vagaries of the expedition's packhorses made up for them. Often the party traveled through such heavy timber that the horses could not be picketed at night because they would become entangled in the trees. Hobbles could be used to limit their wanderings, but a hobbled horse can go a long way between sunset and daybreak, even without the hobbles breaking. If the hobbles did break, it made finding the horses that much more difficult.

Missing horses plagued the party continually. The men were only 2 weeks out when two horses were found to be missing. Hardisty and Pepin were sent after them. Moodie waited until two in the afternoon for their return to camp, and when they did not show up by that time, he could wait no longer. He, Lafferty and Fitzgerald moved camp 6 more miles. Hardisty and Pepin did not come back with the missing horses until 7 p.m. Hardisty explained that the horses had gone back along their old trail and swum the river they had just crossed to return to their last camp.

The next day the same thing happened. Though the men finished breakfast by 6 a.m., they did not get away until 10 a.m. because of the delay caused by searching for their horses in the timber.

Having served at Maple Creek, Saskatchewan, the center of a ranching area, Fitzgerald was well acquainted with the erratic behavior of horses and the problems they can cause. If horses had been the only problem, the trip would have been relatively pleasant.

Muskeg was a bane of their existence. On one occasion they traveled 3 hours through a muskeg in which their horses became mired; only by extreme effort and good fortune were they able to save the horses and keep going. The horses were so exhausted when they worked clear that camp was made at noon, but for the men the day was just beginning. They cut brush and built 5 more miles of trail that afternoon so the horses would have easier going in the morning. This swamp,

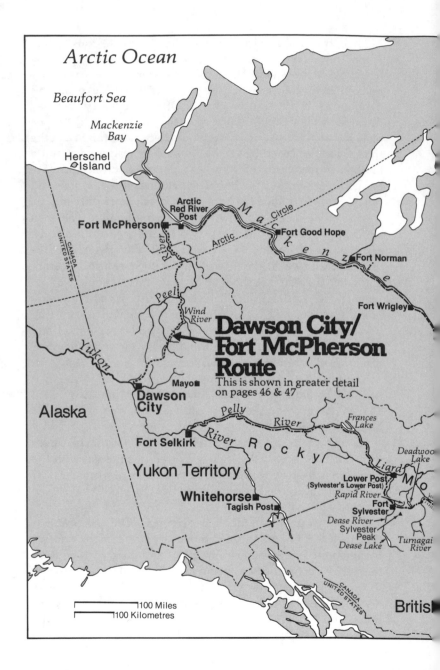

Arctic Ocean

Beaufort Sea

Mackenzie Bay

Herschel Island

Arctic Red River Post

Fort McPherson

Fort Good Hope

Fort Norman

CANADA
UNITED STATES

Peel

Wind River

Fort Wrigley

Dawson City/ Fort McPherson Route
This is shown in greater detail on pages 46 & 47

Yukon

Mayo

Dawson City

Alaska

Pelly

River

Frances Lake

Fort Selkirk

River

R o c k y

Deadwoo Lake

Liard

Yukon Territory

Whitehorse

Tagish Post

Lower Post
(Sylvester's Lower Post)

Rapid River

Fort Sylvester

Dease River

Sylvester Peak

Dease Lake

Turnagai River

CANADA
UNITED STATES

Britis

100 Miles
100 Kilometres

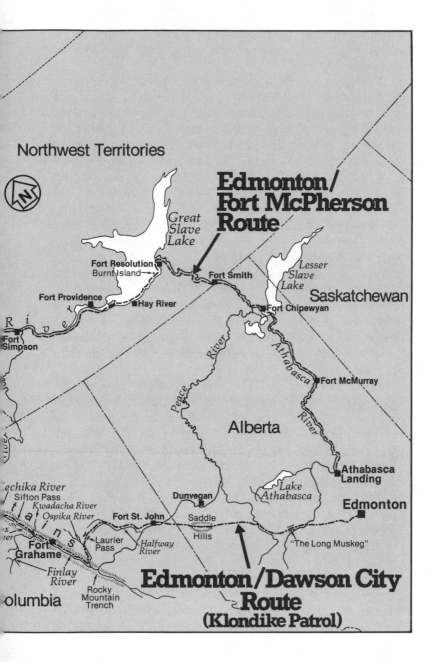

Northwest Territories

**Edmonton/
Fort McPherson
Route**

*Great
Slave
Lake*

Fort Resolution
Burnt Island →

Fort Smith

*Lesser
Slave
Lake*

Saskatchewan

Fort Providence

■Hay River

Fort Chipewyan

R i v e r

Fort
Simpson

Peace River

Athabasca River

■Fort McMurray

Alberta

■Athabasca
Landing

echika River
Sifton Pass
Kwadacha River
Ospika River

Fort St. John

Dunvegan

*Lake
Athabasca*

Edmonton

Saddle
Hills

Laurier
Pass

*Halfway
River*

"The Long Muskeg"

Fort
Grahame

*Finlay
River*

Rocky
Mountain
Trench

olumbia

**Edmonton/Dawson City
Route**
(Klondike Patrol)

15

which earned the title of "The Long Muskeg," is close to the village of Windfall on today's maps, near the town of Whitecourt, Alberta.

Three days after the adventure in the muskeg, Moodie gave his horses another day's rest, but for himself and his men there was no rest. That day they went 8 miles past their camp, making bridges, slashing their way through brush and blazing a trail through burnt and fallen timber. The party took on the semblance of a mini-construction company, where the functions of one hundred men were combined in only six, without the benefit of mechanization. But even at this point, the Mounties were not the first ones over the trail. Almost daily, they leap-frogged parties that had left for the Klondike before them.

Unlike the scattered parties of gold hunters, Inspector Moodie's expedition was the first traveling overland to the Yukon to concern itself completely with the route. They continued to slash their way northwestward. The clouds of mosquitoes that had plagued them when they started the journey were gone by the time they crossed the Little Smoky River, but additional trail problems arose to obstruct their progress.

Timber blown down by storms and heavy snows—commonly called windfall—plagued the men and horses constantly. At some points the men were forced to backtrack when the downed timber became so thick it was impassable. Windfall was so prevalent throughout the expedition that Moodie ultimately referred to it with the abbreviation "D.T." in his diary. The patrol encountered the worst windfall southwest of Dunvegan, in the Saddle Hills area, on October 19. Here they ran into a veritable jungle of heavy fallen timber, which blocked their way on three sides. Since it was near the end of the day, the group was forced to make camp that night without water.

In the process of extricating themselves from this maze, they averaged less than 2 mph over the next 3 days. This time the cantankerous horses were of some help. They strayed from camp the third morning, heading back along the old trail as usual. Fitzgerald, Hardisty and Pepin went looking for them and in the process found a few blazes on trees, indicating that they had ridden right by the trail they had been following. This trail, which was really little more than a series of vague paths going generally in the same direction, had been made by stampeders who had attempted the route from Edmonton before the Moodie expedition was formed.

Another problem was the human factor. Ed Wilson, an American who had come north in 1890, was hired by Moodie to guide the party from a point southwest of Dunvegan to Fort St. John. During the days when the men were hemmed in by windfall, Ed Wilson disappeared. Fitzgerald and Tobin rode ahead to search for him. They ultimately picked up his trail and followed it for half a day, only to have it disappear in a labyrinth of willows. That same day, Fitzgerald and Tobin came down with such severe cases of stomach cramps that they were completely incapacitated. Tobin was so bad that he passed out. This illness, which may have been caused by any number of conditions often found on the trail—too much grease in the food, spoiled food, continual cold, bad water—could also have caused Wilson's demise, as he was never seen again by the Moodie party.

Trouble with guides was a continual headache and may have prejudiced Fitzgerald later against their use. One Indian guide quit because he was afraid of Indians of a different tribe. Another left because he had little faith in the sanity of men who would slash their way through obstacles rather than take the easy way around them. On a number of occasions, guides earned their dismissal through outright incompetence or intransigence. In one case, a métis guide would not hobble his horses, with the result that unnecessary time was spent looking for them. Moodie discharged the man after Fitzgerald reported the man's horses missing several days in a row.

The North-West Mounted Police expedition finally reached the Peace River. Unable to ford it, they built a raft to carry their supplies across. A 5 mph current swept the raft 500 yards downstream, and they had to pull it back upstream with a hand line once they reached the other side. The men swam 10 horses across the river. The other horses would not budge because of the swift current, cold water and a high wind that swept the river. Leaving the remaining horses on the far bank, the Mounties proceeded to Fort St. John and there solicited the assistance of Mr. Gunn of the Hudson's Bay Company. Gunn took his flatbottom riverboat and, with four men at the oars, led the horses across the river using ropes. The last horse nearly drowned in the middle of the river, but Fitzgerald grabbed the horse's mane and head and held it above water until the boat reached shore.

After completing the first leg of the journey at Fort St. John, Moodie had planned to purchase dogs for the next leg, up the Halfway River, but a week earlier he had heard that none were available at Fort St. John. Consequently, he dispatched Hardisty on horseback to see if he could purchase dogs at the Hudson's Bay post at Lesser Slave Lake, 200 miles to the east. Hardisty was successful, and came back up the Peace River by motor vessel with 33 dogs and 5 sleighs.

The month of November saw Inspector Moodie, Fitzgerald and the others of the party preoccupied with their logistical problems. Thirty-three dogs now had to be fed. Since there was hardly enough food for the dogs already at the post, feeding the 33 additions caused considerable strain. The dogs were fed just about anything that was edible. Two days after their arrival, the men mixed dumplings of flour and grease to feed the dogs. A few days later, Fitzgerald picked out a blind horse that was unlikely to be of much use and butchered it, but the meat only amounted to a few hundred pounds, which was not much for 33 dogs. Several days later he purchased a range bull from the Hudson's Bay Company and killed it. The meat was enough to supply the dogs for 2 days and provide 175 pounds of dog food for the trail. Dog food was a never-ending problem. The dogs were needed for transport, but they had to have fuel. In turn, the men had to scramble constantly to feed the dogs so they could pull supplies needed by the men. Often, men and dogs ate the same thing — horse meat. Fitzgerald most certainly learned the logistical problems of handling dogs on this expedition.

Moodie finally resolved the "fuel" problem by deciding to take 15 of his healthiest horses west with the dog teams when they left Fort St. John for the rugged trip over the Rocky Mountains. The horses would be used to pull sleighs as far as practicable, and then would be destroyed to feed the dogs.

Frank Fitzgerald had more than his share of work to do at this point. He had to kill and butcher horses, haggle with squaws over the cost of a hundred mittens for the next leg of the journey, barter with snowshoe makers, search out and cut birch trees for snowshoe frames, build shafts for horses, make dog harnesses and help Inspector Moodie search out and employ dependable men for the trip. Indians Napoleon Thomas and Dick Eggs were hired, as was Tom Sinclair, a white man. All three were shrewd men at the bargaining table, and not only demanded a good salary, but also the guarantee that they would be shipped home by boat if and when the overland expedition reached areas accessible to the Pacific Ocean.

Finally, on December 2, 1897, the party left for Fort Grahame. They slowly worked their way westward into the foothills of the Rocky Mountains, but not without problems. A few days out, a horse delayed the trek for 2½ hours because he bucked himself off balance and fell, breaking one of the shafts of the sleigh. Another time, dissension arose when a cook named Joe Inkster told Moodie he thought Tobin and Lafferty should take their turns lighting the fire in the morning. Inspector Moodie told the man that he was getting paid to cook and not to worry about the others. Later, Moodie wrote in his diary that he was of the opinion that Baptiste Pepin had put the cook up to his rebellion.

The snow became increasingly deep as the men climbed higher into the mountains. By Christmas Day, 1897, they were near the pass at the headwaters of the Halfway River that led to the Ospika River. Here, Baptiste Pepin told Inspector Moodie that if he heard anything about his being dissatisfied, to disregard it. He would go anywhere the inspector wanted him to go. Further, Pepin said that Napoleon Thomas and one of the other men hired for that leg wanted to go home as soon as they reached Fort Grahame. Moodie made provision to accommodate them.

The party drove the horses as far as they could go. On December 29 and 30 they killed six horses, only to find out that Napoleon Thomas had managed to kill two cow moose ahead of them on the trail. Dressing out the horses and moose and then packing the meat from so many animals was no easy task, considering that a single moose or horse quarter may weigh up to two hundred pounds. Executing this simple survival chore must have been an education to the 28-year-old Fitzgerald. In addition, he was getting plenty of experience in working with dog teams, having no less than six teams to supervise as they climbed into the deep snows of the pass over the divide between Halfway River and Ospika River.

The problems of breaking trail through deep snow can never be underestimated in calculating a winter trip in the bush. On one stretch, where it took Moodie and two of his men 4 hours to break a fresh trail, it took the others only an hour and 45 minutes to follow over the newly packed snow.

Shortly after crossing the pass, the men came to a small river which they followed southwest. They had to detour around a mile-long canyon through which the river flowed in impassable rapids, and then the men dropped down into the valley of the Ospika River. They followed the Ospika for 40 miles, continuing in a southerly direction until they reached the Finlay River. They were now presented with a problem familiar to the fisherman, hunter or hiker of today who has parked his car along a road and spent a day in the forest. If he doesn't manage to come back out onto the road at exactly the same spot, in which direction is his car parked? Moodie and the others were at a loss to figure out whether Fort Grahame was upriver or down. The situation was so similar to that which Fitzgerald was to experience on his fatal patrol 13 years later as to be ironic. On this occasion the guide, Napoleon Thomas, faced better odds than the fatal patrol did years later: at least he knew what river he was on, giving him a 50-50 chance to guess right. But Thomas guessed wrong. They went downriver 14 miles before Thomas discovered they were going in the wrong direction. Moodie dispatched Joe Inkster to call back Fitzgerald, who had been breaking trail several miles ahead of the main party. The men retraced their steps back up the Finlay River. They had traveled 28 miles out of their way. Considering the physical torment experienced in breaking trail for even a mile, it must have been maddening to have made such a mistake. Such mistakes when traveling on marginal rations could be costly, as Moodie, Fitzgerald and a chagrined Thomas were soon to find out.

On January 15, the party ran out of dog food, and on the 16th they fed bacon to the dogs. On January 17, they fed the dogs the last of the bacon, and they ran completely out of supplies for both the dogs and themselves that night. They continued north, luckily reaching Fort Grahame the next day. Here they found enough food for the men, but there was not enough to feed the dogs. This was to cause them considerable difficulty and to delay the party for the remainder of the winter. They had traveled 406 miles in 47 days from Fort St. John, including the 28-mile mistake. Temperatures had varied from -45°F to 30°F above. Inspector Moodie now had a critical decision to make. Without food, the dogs would die and his expedition would come to an end. Fitzgerald was chosen to lead a foray to a nearby lake (probably Tomias Lake) to obtain fish for dog food. He purchased hooks and lines from the Hudson's Bay clerk, William Fox, who also lent him nets. Fox told Fitzgerald that the lake was 20 miles southwest.

Several dog teams were lined up to make the trip. Since the dogs were getting weak, everything had to be taken off the sleds except absolute essentials. Fitzgerald left for the lake on January 19. Six days later, he sent in a report that it had taken the weakened dogs 3 days to reach the lake and in 2 days of actual fishing, the party had caught only 17 fish, hardly enough to resupply food used to go to the lake in the first place. Fitzgerald stayed at the lake until February 11.

Inspector Moodie had cached a supply of food back in the pass between the Halfway and Ospika rivers, but he could not use it. He wrote in his diary: *"It is impossible to get our cache down here until I can get a supply of dog feed, and the dogs will have to be fed up before they are fit to work."* It was the old "chicken or the egg" problem all over again.

Unseasonably warm weather did not help things any. On one occasion, Moodie and Fitzgerald went out to retrieve a cache of moose meat and found the trail so heavy that it took them 7¾ hours to go 8 miles. They still had not reached the cache when Fitzgerald volunteered at 10:30 p.m. to continue up the trail to get the meat, part of which was now desperately needed to feed the teams they had with them. Fitzgerald and an Indian lad broke trail for 4 miles, then backpacked a hundred pounds of meat, arriving at camp at 4:15 in the morning. Said Moodie, *"Constable Fitzgerald volunteered for this, as he does for any hard work which is to be done."*

During the months of March and April, it was a continual struggle to obtain food enough for dogs and men. The men ranged far and wide, including a trip along their back trail to a cache they had left behind on their trip from Fort St. John. The snow was 4 to 6 feet deep in the mountains. In many instances the dogs could barely make it up the hills because of the deep snow. Sleds had to be unhitched and the men pulled them up hills with their own hands. Fitzgerald did this so often on this part of the trip that his right hand began to swell up like a chunk of sourdough. The swelling extended to his wrist and had to be continually poulticed. Soon he could not use it at all. Inspector Moodie noted in his diary: *"I think [the swelling] was caused by heavy pulling of ropes, hauling sleighs up hills, as Fox had the same thing in a mild way on his return with us from bringing in the moose."*

Others suffered similar discomforts. On four different occasions, Moodie was afflicted with snow blindness, a notoriously painful condition caused by the glare of the sun off the snow. Lafferty cut his hand, and Tobin was severely injured when a tree branch snapped back, hitting him below the eye and fracturing his cheekbone. This happened on the trail, but did not deter Tobin. He elected to keep going. The injury eventually healed, but to persevere on the trail must have been a great test of his inner strength.

Fitzgerald's steady work on the trip led Inspector Moodie to take him more and more into his confidence in making important decisions. Moodie, Fitzgerald and the Hudson's Bay clerk, William Fox, discussed the situation and decided that the only alternative was for Moodie to go south to Stuart Lake for supplies, leaving Fitzgerald in charge at Fort Grahame. While Moodie was away from April 1 to July 7, 1898, with Lafferty, Tobin, Pepin and Napoleon Thomas, Fitzgerald backtracked over the trail to Fort St. John to observe it without snow, and wrote a lengthy report as to conditions and navigability for packtrains and carts.

The interval the Mounties spent at Fort Grahame had not been without its compensations, at least as far as the preservation of law and order went. This function of the Mounties had been all but lost in the maze of other duties the men of the patrol were performing. Fitzgerald's presence through the winter and spring helped keep the Indians of the area from staging a revolt. They had good reason for their strong feelings: white men heading to the Klondike were shooting the game the Indians normally hunted to stay alive. During that winter the problem became so acute that the Indians threatened to charge a toll on 11 parties going through their land. If they were not paid, they said, they would kill the white men's horses, and even the men if they did not leave.

Fitzgerald advised the Natives that they would surely be wiped out if such a confrontation occurred. Tactfully, he suggested that the Indians wait for the return of Inspector Moodie, who could then inform the central government of their plight. The Natives agreed, and a skirmish was avoided.

There were also occasional nasty incidents between whites, as cabin fever took its toll. Most of the whites were well equipped with firearms. Consequently, when an argument started, threats to settle disputes with their weapons were hurled about with considerable abandon. On more than one occasion, Fitzgerald had to confront the antagonists with the prospect of going to jail. In this way, Fitzgerald kept the peace until Moodie returned and the expedition started north again.

Chapter 3
Klondike Patrol: Fort Grahame to the Yukon

On July 15, 1898, after a period of 6 months during which the party had not gained one step north (although its members had probably traveled over two thousand miles in other directions), Inspector Moodie, Fitzgerald and the others finally set out toward Sylvester Landing on the Dease River.

As if in tribute to the men who had struggled so much since the preceding September, Mother Nature now offered them easier going as they traveled up the trough of the Rocky Mountain Trench.

They met several parties camped at the confluence of the Finlay, Fox and Kwadacha rivers, and here they learned that their work had not been in vain; swarms of stampeders were following the trail the Mounties had so laboriously slashed the previous fall. Moodie mentioned in his diary meeting George Adsit, who told the inspector that he and his companion had left Edmonton April 12 and reached Fort St. John on May 20, following the Mounties' trail. Adsit covered the distance in half the time it took the Mounties. Adsit and his companion, who had started from Montana, traveled light; Moodie noted that they carried less than 150 pounds of supplies each. Judging by the fast time the two men had made, they were obviously trail-hardened long before they headed into the bush from Edmonton.

The good weather held as the Mounties descended the Kechika River north of Sifton Pass, though, as usual, nature had its share of tricks to play. In wilderness travel, it seems that every piece of good luck has to be balanced by an accompanying drawback. This time good weather meant forest fires. At one lunch stop, a wall of flame swept down upon them when about half the horses were unpacked and they had to make for the river, abandoning the packs still on the ground. In his haste, Moodie forgot his valuable notes, which were in his valise. If the notes went up in smoke, it would wipe out one whole segment of their survey of the route between Fort Grahame and their present camp. Moodie raced back on foot in an attempt to retrieve his valise. As the flames swept down on the camp, it looked like it would be a futile effort. However, the fickleness of the wilderness again came into play. The wind suddenly changed, sweeping the flames away and saving Moodie's notes.

With the exception of the area swept by the fire, the country through which the men were going was prolific with meadows and grass, with a breath-taking panorama of rugged mountains that extended northward on either side of the trench as far as the eye could see. On August 11, Moodie noted: *"This afternoon's travel has been almost without a break, through magnificent feed, and for the last hour we have traversed as fine a summer range for stock as could be desired."* Such description was the rule rather than the exception during this segment of the trip.

Few words can adequately describe this vast land extending from Sifton Pass to the Dease River. There are areas that comprise a summer range which has never been grazed since Moodie, Fitzgerald and the stampeders went through; this country today is as virginal and vacant as it was then, with but few settlers. An irascible old packer, Skook Davidson, who formerly ran an isolated ranch in this area, had so many horses running half wild that he said, in a letter to the author, *"I just don't know how many I got."*

Moodie and his men plodded down the Kechika to the

Turnagain River, went up this a short distance and then struck out west over an old pack trail to Deadwood Lake. From there they continued west to the Rapid River, then to Sylvester Landing on the Dease River, near the junction of McDame Creek with the Dease.

Sylvester Landing, now McDame, was originally named for Rufus Sylvester, an early trader who established the post in 1876 to serve the placer miners on McDame Creek. At the time of the Moodie patrol, the post lay on a route from Telegraph Creek to the headwaters of the Pelly River, via the Liard River and Frances Lake.

Moodie's party reached Sylvester in the middle of August, only to run into the old problem of supplies. The Hudson's Bay post had been swept clean by the stampeders, leaving the Mounties no alternative but to purchase sufficient flour, beans and bacon from other parties camped in the area to fill out their larder for the dash to their destination. The big problem Inspector Moodie now faced was getting through to the Pelly before freezeup; a delay at the headwaters of the river could make several months' difference in the arrival of the patrol at Fort Selkirk, located at the confluence of the Yukon and Pelly rivers. Such a delay could also create hardships that might endanger their lives. At least the route ahead was known: it had been mapped in detail by George M. Dawson of the Geological Survey of Canada in 1887.

The North-West Mounted Police expedition left for the Pelly on August 24. Theirs was the last party to leave Fort Sylvester for Frances Lake that season, as all of the others who arrived there while Moodie and his men were camped at the post decided either to go out by way of Glenora, or to winter at Dease Lake.

It took the Mounties 2 months to reach the Pelly River. During the trip they had to purchase a canoe from three prospectors. They also built a raft, after abandoning their horses to local guides, and reached the confluence of the Macmillan and Pelly rivers on October 17. Three days downriver they ran into an 8-mile ice jam. A heavy rain squall struck the party at the same time. Moodie ordered the canoe cached and he, Fitzgerald and the others walked the last 40 miles down the Pelly to its junction with the Yukon, arriving on October 24.

Local woodcutters ferried them across the Yukon River to Fort Selkirk where they were greeted by Colonel Evans of the Yukon Field Force. Inspector Moodie instructed one of the Mounties stationed at the post to pick up the cached canoe and supplies as soon as the river froze. Luckily, the Yukon River was still open and the next morning Moodie and the others (except for Tobin, who decided to spend the winter at Dawson City) took passage on the *Ora*, the last steamer for Whitehorse. From Whitehorse the party made their way by canoe, steamer and packstring to Skagway, arriving there on November 6. Moodie and Fitzgerald returned to Maple Creek on November 20.

Constable Fitzgerald had performed his duties with considerable perseverance. Inspector Moodie did not fail to point out the excellence of Fitzgerald's attitude. Moodie was so impressed by his service that he twice mentioned to his superiors that he thought Fitzgerald would make a fine noncommissioned officer, and soon after he was promoted to sergeant.

Fitzgerald's service with the Mounties, however, was due for a temporary curtailment. The Boer War had begun, and many men from Canada rushed to the colors. One of these recruits was Francis Fitzgerald. He was so eager to go that he went through a painful experience out of fear that he might be left out of the conflict.

A few days prior to his enlistment, he broke his little toe when he tripped over the guy-rope of a tent. It was a bad break, with the toe projecting at a right angle to his foot. He pulled the bone straight and splinted it. The next day, he walked several miles with the boot off his foot, and when he neared the place of enlistment, he took the homemade splint off his toe and shoved his foot into the boot. He then walked into the place of enlistment without a limp. He was afraid the army might turn him down or delay him so that he would not be able to accompany his friends who were joining at the same time.

He enlisted as a sergeant on January 5, 1900, in the 2nd Canadian Mounted Rifles. The unit was commanded by L. W. Herchmer, formerly Commissioner of the Mounties, and the majority of the officers and NCOs also came from the Mounties. After a year in action in South Africa, Fitzgerald, with his unit, was relieved and returned to Canada in January 1901. When he arrived in Halifax, Fitzgerald was one of nine men given accolades in the local newspapers. He was discharged from the army on January 14, 1901. At this time he became engaged to Mary Shepard, a local girl. In fact, they never became disengaged, but the girl could hardly know or understand that her fiance's soul was already captured by a rival of uncompromising nature and lasting allure—the vast land of the Northern forests.

Fitzgerald could have bought his way out of the North-West Mounted Police if he had wished. Or he could have requested his fiancée to accompany him on his Northern sojourns, but then, quite possibly he realized that a land where mosquitoes were thicker than clouds of dust in summer, and where in winter the mercury dipped to -75°F was no place for a city-bred girl. At any rate, he did not marry her and he did not take her North.

One of history's minor tragic romances was the result. After his promotion to inspector, Fitzgerald became involved with an Eskimo girl named Lena Oonalina. He requested permission to marry her, but was turned down by his superiors. A child was born of that relationship in August, 1909, and was named Annie. She was baptized by the Reverend W. H. Fry at Herschel Island on August 1, 1912. Annie had suffered a crippling injury at birth, however, and died at 18 at Hay River. Lena later married an Eskimo named Ambrose and moved to the Coronation Gulf district.

It was not long after his return to Canada that Fitzgerald was to head "down North" to Herschel Island.

Chapter 4
Fitzgerald at Herschel Island

After his return from the Boer War, Frank Fitzgerald was again assigned to his old post at Maple Creek. However, in the spring of 1903 he was given the new Herschel Island-Fort McPherson command. Superintendent Charles Constantine was to join him on the trek north to oversee the establishment of the new posts and to make an on-the-spot evaluation of the situation in the Arctic. He would then leave Fitzgerald in command and depart for the south. On the trip north they were accompanied by Constables S. S. Munroe, F. D. Sutherland, R. H. Walker, John Galpin and Special Constable Joseph Belrose.

The Mounties set out from Athabasca Landing (present-day Athabasca) in bateaux on May 26, traveling in two separate parties for the first leg of the long journey. Fitzgerald, Munroe, Sutherland and Walker went through and around the rugged rapids of the Athabasca River, where they met one of the best canoe men ever seen on that river. This man, Ladoucier, would paddle a canoe through some of the most dangerous rapids on the river. His technique was to stand up in the stern in order to better see the water that lay ahead. (Rather than have his passengers risk the hazardous journey through the white water, he would ask them to walk around the rapids.) Quieter water was reached at Fort McMurray, where the two parties met briefly on June 7.

On June 9, Fitzgerald, Galpin, Munroe and Belrose loaded their gear onto a Hudson's Bay bateau and, towed by a tug, headed downriver. They arrived at Fort Chipewyan, where they had to wait for Superintendent Constantine and his group who, traveling by flatboat, had been held up by stiff headwinds at the 12-mile crossing of the western end of Lake

Athabasca. The entire party was finally reunited; their only losses were a canoe being freighted on one of the flatboats and the police skiff at Chipewyan.

The superintendent noted that Fort Chipewyan was in a state of decay; the buildings were out of repair and the entire post appeared dilapidated. During the time Fitzgerald, Constantine and the rest of the party were there, they met an influx of Indians who had journeyed from throughout the North Country to the settlement to collect treaty money. About this time, Belrose, who had acted as interpreter, was sent back to his regular post at Lesser Slave Lake.

They were delayed here until all the freight for downriver was portaged to Fort Smith. Finally the police party, with the exception of Constantine who had gone ahead, left from Fort Smith aboard the *Wrigley*, a screw steamer of 96 tons. They went down the Slave River to Fort Resolution on Great Slave Lake, arriving there on July 5. Superintendent Constantine rejoined them there. That night they started across Great Slave Lake, but a severe storm drove them to shelter in the lee of Burnt Island, 14 miles from Resolution. When the storm let up, they pointed the *Wrigley* toward Hay River and arrived there the next day.

The next stage of the trip saw the *Wrigley* sail from Great Slave Lake down the Mackenzie River to Fort Providence, where the first Hudson's Bay post on the river was located. After a brief stop, they continued on, and by July 10 arrived at Fort Simpson. Even in the year 1903, technology's fingers were reaching into the North Country: Fort Simpson had a sawmill run by an engine that also generated electricity for an electric light.

The Hudson's Bay boat now made fast time downriver, stopping briefly at Fort Wrigley, Fort Norman and Fort Good Hope on the journey to Fort McPherson, which they reached on July 14, 1903.

McPherson was located on the right limit of the Peel River, about 30 miles above the junction of the Peel with the Mackenzie River. Five Hudson's Bay Company buildings, in tumble-down condition with the exception of the dwelling house, plus the house of the missionary, a church and a few Indian huts greeted the Mounties when they stepped ashore.

Constantine was fortunate in being able to rent several vacant buildings for his men at $45 for 3 months. In one building there were three large rooms, 18 by 24 feet. The building was suitable for a storehouse where food would be safe from the cold.

Fitzgerald, after seeing the first of the two posts in which he was to winter, could not have been overwhelmed with pleasure at the prospect. Fort McPherson was the picture of desolation. The superintendent reported that the sur-roundings were not very pleasant: with the village hemmed in by the river in front and small lakes and swamps behind, it looked cold and inhospitable. Worse still was the high bank that separated the town from the river. The supply boat had to anchor in the middle of the river, and rowboats were used to carry goods ashore. Then the supplies had to be packed up a 200-foot-high bank to the Hudson's Bay warehouse. The same thing had to be done with wood, which was a necessity during the long cold winters. The town was overrun with dogs, and no one cleaned up after them.

A band of Indians had just come in from a winter in the mountains of the upper Porcupine and Peel rivers. They told Fitzgerald and Constantine that Fort Yukon was about 8 days away, depending on how fast one could make it over the Stony Creek portage to the Bell River, down which one could raft to Fort Yukon. It took another few days to go up the Yukon River to Dawson City. That was the summer route. The Indians reported it took 16 days in winter by another route, but were rather vague as to its location.

Constantine's observations of Fort McPherson as a practical place for a police post were ironic in view of the ultimate sequence of events that led to the death of the men of the Lost Patrol. Significantly, he saw no use in building a post in a place he considered of little strategic importance for the Mounties' purposes. Constantine expressed the opinion that a year would finish the usefulness of the McPherson post. His reasoning was based on newly received reports that the whalers, and Natives attracted by their presence, had left Herschel Island. He suggested that the best way to police the Arctic coast was by a revenue cutter service, similar to that used by the Americans farther to the west. Communications with the outside world could be fixed by arranging a summer rendezvous at which a patrol from Dawson City would meet a patrol from the revenue cutter.

The superintendent instructed Fitzgerald to ascertain the best route for such a meeting, at the same time making sure all those involved traveled only through Canadian territory. He went on to point out that communication via the Mackenzie River was impracticable. The nearest post to McPherson (other than the Hudson's Bay Company post at Arctic Red River, which was some 30 miles away) was Fort Good Hope, 284 miles away. In winter, deep snows made it impossible to keep a series of trails open the entire length of the Mackenzie River. In summer, paddling and tracking a canoe up the river was impractical for purposes of communication because of the great distance involved.

"I would recommend that next summer the detachment at McPherson be withdrawn, if the present conditions existing in that portion of the territory continue," said Constantine. He suggested that the detachment be divided, with one NCO and two constables being sent to Fort Simpson, and two constables to Fort Resolution.

Constantine's observations were quite practical, considering that the only other Mountie post in that part of the North Country was at Fort Chipewyan.

Fitzgerald's orders from Constantine were to make a patrol as soon as possible to Herschel Island. The primary purpose

33

for this was to determine if the initial reasons for establishing a detachment at Fort McPherson were still valid. Were the whalers still using the island? Were there Eskimos living there? Did it look like the Americans might lay claim to the island?

Fitzgerald remained at Fort McPherson only 2 weeks before leaving for Herschel Island. Constantine had already departed for the south. Accompanying Fitzgerald was Constable Sutherland and an interpreter named Thompson. It took them 10 days to make the 260-mile trip to Herschel in a mission whaleboat.

The itinerant sergeant was used to out-of-the-way places, but Herschel Island strained even his sense of the absurd. He found the island to be without a tree or shrub, and reported that all fuel had to be brought from the mainland in winter by dog team and in the summer by boat.

There was a total of six buildings on the island. Four were owned by the Pacific Steam Whaling Company. Of the four, one was loaned to the Anglican mission as a dwelling, and the other three were storehouses for the company. A fifth building was owned by a whaling captain named McKenna, and the last one was owned by the Anglican mission. In addition to these, there were 15 sod huts. *"These,"* wrote Fitzgerald, *"are owned by the Pacific Steam Whaling Company and are used in the winter by the officers of the whalers, who nearly all keep a Native woman . . ."*

Sergeant Fitzgerald found out that, contrary to reports received by Constantine, Herschel Island had not been abandoned by the whalers. Not only were there buildings, there were ships, two having wintered there with 67 men. These were the *Narwhal* and the *Olga*. In addition, six whaling ships arrived between August 16 and 19 and unloaded supplies. A somewhat frustrated Fitzgerald reported that he could not collect any customs duties because he had not yet received tariff schedules.

One of the first tasks Fitzgerald performed was to investigate the reported liquor problem on the island. He had been told that the Natives would go on a roaring drunk on the beach as soon as the whalers reached Herschel each year. He warned captains of the whaling ships against giving and trading liquor to the Eskimos. The only goods traded this year were in return for work done by the Natives, as they had had a poor year trapping.

The sergeant's first confrontation over liquor occurred when a Native woman obtained a bottle and became drunk and unruly. He confined the woman while he searched her house, where he found the bottle and broke it. In another incident he sentenced a Native man to 2 days' confinement for drinking. He told the culprit that he would have locked him up for 30 days but for the fact that he had to make a trip to Fort McPherson. Of the incident, Fitzgerald said almost apologetically, *"I had to sentence him; if I did not, it would have no effect on them."*

After journeying to Fort McPherson and remaining there for a brief period, Fitzgerald realized that most of the activity would be at Herschel Island. Consequently, he made arrangements with Reverend Whittaker, the missionary, for transportation for himself and his supplies back to Herschel. On his return, he purchased five tons of coal at $20 a ton from the S.S. *Baylies*, and also bought two sod huts and a storehouse for his winter quarters.

In writing of the situation at Herschel that first year of the Mounties' occupation of the island, the sergeant said he had only four sheets of paper on which to write the report, there being not a scrap on the island.

Fitzgerald's assignment was probably as difficult as any given to an officer of comparable rank that year. He was about as far northwest from headquarters in Regina as he could get and still be in Canada. He and two constables were responsible for dealing with a predominantly alien population at Herschel, and they had the vast Arctic Coast and lower Mackenzie River areas under their jurisdiction as well. They had relatively primitive living conditions at the island, and little better at Fort McPherson. Fitzgerald had no adequate means of communicating with his superiors; consequently, the responsibility for making decisions affecting forty thousand square miles of territory rested on his shoulders alone. He not only had to perform a Mountie's duties, but also those of a customs' agent, diplomat and health inspector. (Toward the end of his sojourn at Herschel Island, Fitzgerald was also appointed mining inspector.) The one exception to this isolation was the annual Dawson City patrol which provided a means of delivering Fitzgerald's reports to his superiors. It would have taken more than a year to receive an answer to any question he might pose. He was to earn a promotion to inspector for his superlative handling of this difficult assignment.

The normal number of afflictions and accidents occurred while Fitzgerald was at Herschel. When Inspector Jarvis arrived on an inspection tour of the post in 1908, he found Fitzgerald, now a Staff Sergeant, suffering from an acute attack of the flu, but the sergeant would not go off duty.

By this time, Constable Sam Carter had joined Fitzgerald at Herschel. Jarvis said of Carter: *"Constable Carter is an excellent cook, and I know him of old to be a good dog driver . . ."*

Carter met with a painful accident one day while setting fishnets on the Peel River. Reaching out from his boat to catch hold of a buoy while going downstream, the strength of the current and weight of the boat forced his arm back and tore the muscles. He must have suffered considerably, because there were few medicines on the island, and what they did have was a skimpy supply obtained from the whalers.

No less than 20 white men had been buried at Herschel Island by the year 1908, and there were others who had died on Herschel but were not buried there. A Captain Wicks had his side crushed falling down the hatch of the *Thrasher*, after which he only lived 2 hours. His body was frozen and taken to San Francisco. Twelve men had been frozen to death at Herschel since 1893, several of these after going through the ice while driving dogs.

There were a number of marriages between whites and Eskimos, and others between Eskimos, one of which involved a beautiful girl of 17. She had had both her feet amputated 3 years earlier, but this apparently did not affect her ability to land a husband. Fitzgerald and Inspector Jarvis were invited to the wedding breakfast, which consisted of seal meat, muktuk (whale meat), and rotten frozen fish. The two tried their best to get into the hut of the bridal couple, but Jarvis reported that the overflowing crowd of 50 people and the odor of the place combined to drive them off.

By the time Jarvis visited the detachment, the Mounties' living quarters had improved considerably over the sod huts they had first lived in. He found the buildings to be comfortable and commodious. They even had a dining room and a billiard room with a partition covered with calico that had been obtained from one of the ships. Fitzgerald was allowed to sleep in an officer's house adjoining the Mountie barracks. The kitchen and bedroom walls were papered, and there were even carpets in the dining room and bedroom.

Inspector Jarvis felt that Fitzgerald was doing an excellent job at his post. He said, *"The discipline of the detachment is all that could be desired. Staff Sergeant Fitzgerald is a capable and efficient noncommissioned officer, with an abundance of tact in handling both whalers and natives."*

The mention of Fitzgerald's tact tends to belie some reports that surfaced after his death that he was a martinet who ruled his men with an iron hand. He was, however, a no-nonsense individual who did his duty as he saw fit.

The sergeant had several important cases to handle while he was at Herschel, one involving a Captain Christian Klengenberg. The captain was charged with the murder of Jackson D. Paul, engineer of the gasoline schooner *Olga*, at Prince Albert Peninsula, on or about September 1, 1905. A warrant was issued for Klengenberg's arrest, but he was apprehended by a United States revenue cutter at Kotzebue Sound, Alaska, and taken to San Francisco for trial. Jarvis noted that Klengenberg had intended to return to Prince Albert Peninsula, and that if he had, Fitzgerald would have gone there to apprehend him.

A second incident was of considerable importance because

of its international implications. It involved Vilhjalmur Stefansson, an anthropologist studying the Northern Eskimo. Stefansson's 1908 expedition was being financed by the Canadian Government and the American Museum of Natural History. Accompanying Stefansson was Dr. R. M. Anderson, who planned to study the fauna of the region. They had also agreed to set up a number of meteorological stations for the Dominion Meteorological Service. The two men traveled very light, only taking with them what equipment and arms were needed to live off the land. They carried no food supplies. Their reason for this was that they planned to join the Eskimos, to live and hunt with them and to obtain their food in that manner.

As happens on occasion, overlooking a small item may have important consequences for an expedition in the wilderness. In this case, it was the omission of matches that was to cause a dispute which was heard all the way back in Ottawa and New York before it had run its course. Stefansson had forgotten matches. Without them, he felt that his party of two white men and nine Eskimos could not get through the winter of 1908-9. As far as he was personally concerned, he felt that a supply of a thousand matches offered by Captain James Wing of the *Karluk* was enough, but Dr. Anderson and several of the Eskimos, who were smokers, refused to head east to winter without a much larger supply. Stefansson then waited for ships that were supposed to arrive with some supplies, but they failed to show up. As a last resort, he pleaded with the sergeant to furnish him with matches, which Fitzgerald refused to do.

Fitzgerald based his refusal on a number of reasons, the primary one being to keep Stefansson and his companions from getting into a starvation situation where they might not only need to be rescued, but could also be a burden on Natives in the area where they were wintering. He tactfully offered Stefansson and Anderson the use of a cabin and supplies if they would remain at Herschel Island for the winter, but he would not back down on his stand not to give them matches. Stefansson saw the futility of further argument and left Herschel Island a few days later to sail west to Point Barrow. There he eventually purchased not only matches, but enough food to last him through the winter. He rationalized his purchase of food by saying it was a necessity because of the relative scarcity of game in the western Arctic as compared to the Mackenzie area. Fitzgerald's superiors were apparently satisfied with his handling of the incident. (See Appendix E for Stefansson's comments on the incident and on Fitzgerald's death.)

Besides confrontations with scientists, the commanders of the isolated posts of the North also had to deal with the usual problems of inclement weather, starvation of the Natives and hazards of travel. The winter of 1908-9 was one of the hardest felt by the Natives on the coast in a number of years because the whaling supply ships did not get in. This tended to underscore observations that the Natives had become overly dependent on the white men. However, there were other reasons why the Eskimos went hungry that had nothing to do with the white man. The extreme cold froze the ice solid around Herschel Island, and it became extremely dangerous for hunters to venture long distances in search of open water because at any time the ice pack could move away from the coast and break up with them on it.

Fitzgerald explained in one of his reports that there were many caribou in the mountains that winter, but the Kogmollick Eskimos of the area were unaccustomed to killing land animals. There were 47 Eskimos on Herschel Island. Fitzgerald found one family with 15 seals, a second family with 2, and none among the remaining families. A number of Eskimos had to boil sealskins for food. Help had to be sent to three families at Kay Point, on the mainland about 23 miles to the southeast. One family found it necessary to eat all of their dogs on the way to Herschel Island. The Natives of the Mackenzie Delta ran out of fish in March, but the sergeant reported that they believed they could get through the rest of the winter subsisting on rabbits and what little fish they could catch.

No ship wintered anywhere in the North that year, with the

exception of the *Rosie H*, which was at Flaxman Island, Alaska, in April. That ship had lost its first mate, who froze to death in a blizzard that ripped the coast on January 1. This same blizzard blew the stovepipes from the roofs of the houses at Herschel, and most of them were never seen again. It also blew away the snow that was banked around the houses for insulation. It had to be shoveled back. A typical temperature fluctuation in the area, recorded by Fitzgerald on December 21, 1908, showed a temperature of 22°F at 7 p.m., and 5 hours later, -52°F, for a total drop of 74 degrees.

Fitzgerald went on a much-deserved home leave in the summer of 1910. During this time he spent an interval in Toronto on recruiting duty for the Royal North-West Mounted Police. He probably stayed with his brother, J. W. Fitzgerald, a salesman, who lived at 14 Sackville Place. He signed up no less than 105 men while assigned to this task.

He visited his widowed mother, Mrs. John Fitzgerald, in Halifax while on leave, and it was at this time that he received the news of his promotion to the rank of inspector. He was 40 years old. He remained east, visiting a number of sisters and cousins who also lived in Halifax, and returned to Herschel Island in the fall.

Two of the men who were to accompany Fitzgerald on the fatal patrol 4 months later—Constables Sam Carter and G. F. Kinney—remained posted at Herschel Island while he was on leave. Fitzgerald had nothing but good words to say about both men. He said in a report that they were both willing workers who never lost their tempers, and added that that was saying a lot in view of the isolation of their post, where reading matter lasted little more than a month.

The hazards of travel were ever present for the men at Northern posts. Staying alive in the Arctic, even when conditions appeared to be moderate, could be a marginal proposition at times, as Fitzgerald found out on several trips between Herschel Island and Fort McPherson. Any change of weather brought complications. On one occasion, he and two others got caught in a storm off the coast while paddling a 14-foot canoe. Unusually large waves battered the fragile craft, and only through extreme luck were they able to reach the safety of land. Capsizing in waters as frigid as those of the Arctic seas was tantamount to sudden death. On another journey, a combination of circumstances resulted in Fitzgerald and Sergeant S.E.A. Selig almost starving on a springtime trip from Herschel Island to McPherson, when the two men ran out of food while sailing a whaleboat up the Mackenzie River. But for the providence of a favorable wind change and the passage of an Indian who gave them food, the Mounties would have experienced considerable discomfort before reaching their destination.

Frank Fitzgerald took these adverse experiences in stride. He appeared to be a philosophical man who adjusted well to his surroundings, and he was not without a sense of humor. On the trip with Sergeant Selig, the pair ran out of tea, and used the last potful of leaves over and over again. He remarked that though tea was not indispensable, it was really not appreciated until one was reduced to drinking muddy river water.

There was little that Inspector Fitzgerald had not experienced in the way of rugged trail travel before his fatal patrol of 1910-11.

Chapter 5
The Route to Fort McPherson

The creation of Mounted Police posts at Herschel Island and Fort McPherson necessitated establishment of a communications route to headquarters at Regina, Saskatchewan. In 1903, Superintendent Constantine, who had foreseen the problem, asked Sergeant Fitzgerald to investigate the alternatives. Constantine's idea of policing the Arctic coast by a revenue cutter service was not, apparently, taken up by his superiors.

There were a number of routes available, but each had drawbacks that discouraged their use. Messages and letters could even be sent from Herschel Island via whaling ships over the sea route, but for the Mounties to send confidential reports concerning the whaling fleet by way of the same fleet was not an ideal situation. In addition, being American, the ships terminated their voyages in foreign ports, which put them out of Canadian jurisdiction.

The Mackenzie route could conceivably be used in the summer and it was inside Canadian territory. However, as Superintendent Constantine had pointed out to Sergeant Fitzgerald, this was as unsatisfactory in summer as in winter because of the great distance.

The communications route, then, obviously would have to connect with Dawson City in the Yukon Territory, as Dawson, closer than any other Canadian community with a Mounted Police unit, had good telegraph and mail connections with southern Canada. There was only one way to get to Dawson City without going through American territory, and that was by way of the Peel River and its tributaries. Two routes were available, one of which had been used by the stampeders in the 1898 gold rush. This went up the Peel and

Wind rivers to the headwaters of the Stewart River, down that river to the Yukon and on to Dawson City. The other route went up the Wind to the Little Wind River and then southwest across several mountain passes to Dawson. The latter was the one finally chosen.

Fitzgerald's recommendations undoubtedly included this route, but a decision was made by higher authorities to have the patrols approach from the south rather than the north, thus taking the planning out of Fitzgerald's hands. The reason for this was that it was more practical to supply a patrol at a division headquarters like Dawson City than to outfit one at such a far-flung post as Fort McPherson, where all supplies were at a premium. The lot fell to B Division at Dawson City. From the time the Mountie patrols started making the annual trip to Fort McPherson in 1904 until the patrols ended in 1921, there was only one patrol that did not set out from Dawson City, and that was Fitzgerald's fatal patrol of 1910-11. Significantly, the quality of his food supplies was a factor in the loss of the patrol.

Besides supplies, it fell to the Dawson City division to obtain guides to lead the Mountie patrols over the new route. Those sought for the job were the Loucheux Indians, nomadic Athabascans who had wandered for centuries through the upper Peel country, hunting, trapping and fishing.

These people were called by whites *Kutchin*, which means "people from a distant place." (Paradoxically, *Kutchin* to a Loucheux means "white people.") The colloquial term "Loucheux" was applied to these Indians of the Northern Yukon by voyageurs in the early 1800s. The term is French for "slant-eyed" people. The Loucheux inhabited a region

43

stretching from the Mackenzie Delta on the east to the upper Chandalar in Alaska on the west. The hunting ground of this mountain band was the area through which the Mountie patrols were to pass. These farthest-north Indians in North America have survived through the centuries in one of the coldest regions on earth. Temperatures of -70°F are common where they live, and -80°F is not unknown.

The Loucheux are generally a friendly people, willing to accommodate strangers in need, at least to the limit of their resources. They first met white men during the explorations of Sir Alexander Mackenzie in 1789. Following Mackenzie were Sir John Franklin, Thomas Simpson, Sir John Richardson and John Bell. In 1840, Bell established a Hudson's Bay Company trading post at Fort McPherson. His reason for establishing the post was the fact that the Loucheux would congregate there after spending the winters trapping in as prolific a high-quality fur area as can be found in the North. This included the upper reaches of the Peel and its tributaries. Prime marten, mink, otter, white fox, wolf, wolverine, weasel, beaver, muskrat and lynx were brought in by the Indians for purchase by the Hudson's Bay Company traders.

Both Catholic and Protestant missionaries followed the traders, with the Roman Catholic faith taking hold in the Arctic Red River village and the Anglican missionary eventually securing a firm foothold at Fort McPherson. By the turn of the century, Archdeacon Robert McDonald of the Anglican Church established St. Mathew's Mission on the Peel River. He developed a syllabic system by which he translated the *Book of Common Prayer* into Loucheux in 1885 and the complete *Bible* in 1898. He taught the Natives English, and consequently by 1900 many of them could read and write, among them, Richard Martin, who was born in 1880, and his younger brother, John, who was born in 1882. Richard was to guide the first Mountie patrol from Dawson City to Fort McPherson via the Hart River-Little Wind River route in 1904, and his brother John was to guide more of these lengthy patrols than any other man.

Their uncle was Colin Vitisik, whose cabin was to be a

refuge for the Mountie patrols for many years. Colin figures prominently in the history of the Loucheux at the turn of the century. George Mitchell, a gold seeker, recalled in his book, *The Golden Grindstone,* that Colin was sort of the wise man of the Peel River people when Mitchell and his companions spent the winter of 1898-9 with the Loucheux. He said Colin, then about 60 years old, was a devout Christian who would read aloud from the *Bible* to those Indians who could not read. They seemed to enjoy hearing the old man, and he was held in great favor and respect by the others. It was at Colin's cabin that Inspector Fitzgerald cached the Lost Patrol's dispatch bag on his desperate struggle for survival in 1911.

Mitchell's party had been caught by the freezeup in the fall of 1898 about 8 miles up the Wind River from its junction with the Peel. They built a little village of cabins, which they called Wind City, and settled in for the winter. This was done despite advice given to them by the Indians that there was a route the stampeders could take across country to Dawson City, with good prospects of arriving there within 10 days. This was the Little Wind River route, which the Mounties later followed. Mitchell said his party did not attempt the route because the majority of the white men congregated there simply did not trust the Indians.

This mistrust was to manifest itself in the death of seven of the men through starvation and scurvy. The survivors generally agreed that more of them would have died but for the fact that the Indians showed up with caribou meat when it was desperately needed.

The Loucheux people demonstrated their friendly nature another time, when they nursed Mitchell back to health after he badly cut his kneecap while chopping wood. It was Colin's wife, Jane, and the wife of Chief Francis, a woman by the name of Flora, who successfully operated on Mitchell's knee to restore it to good health.

Other Loucheux helped the Mitchell expedition during the winter of 1898-9 by taking them food and delivering letters to Fort McPherson. Many of these men were uncles and fathers of Loucheux guides—such as Andrew Kunnizzi, Peter

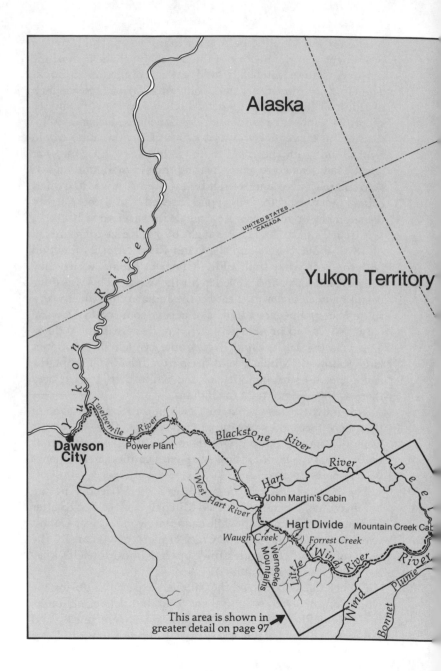

This area is shown in greater detail on page 97

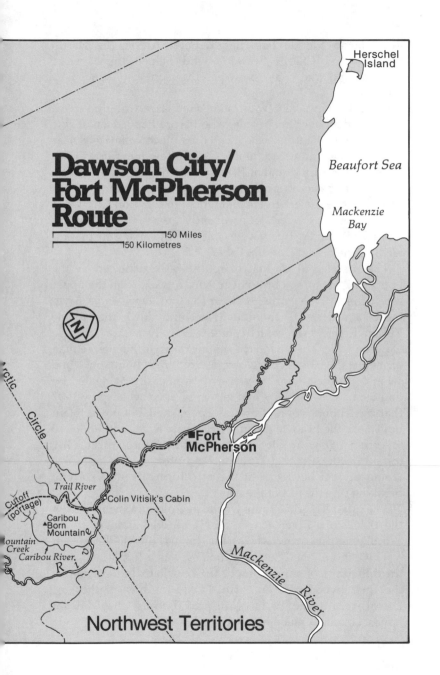

Dawson City/ Fort McPherson Route

50 Miles
50 Kilometres

Herschel Island

Beaufort Sea

Mackenzie Bay

Arctic Circle

Fort McPherson

Trail River

Colin Vitisik's Cabin

Cutoff (portage)

Caribou Born Mountain

Mountain Creek

Caribou River

R i

Mackenzie River

Northwest Territories

Ross, Jacob Njootli, Sam Smith, Peter Alexie, the Martin brothers and Charlie Stewart—who helped the Mountie patrols find the way between Dawson City and Fort McPherson.

Once Dawson City was established as a trading center, many of the Loucheux people, who before had led a nomadic life, elected to settle permanently in places relatively near Dawson, such as at Moosehide, only a few miles downriver from Dawson City, and at Blackstone Village. Using Moosehide as a base of operations, they would trap on the Blackstone and Hart rivers and return to Dawson City when the season was over. Consequently, when the Mounties looked for guides, they were able to find many in the immediate vicinity of Dawson City.

The first leg of the patrol route was established by the Loucheux when they brought furs in to trade from the upper Blackstone River, through Seela Pass to Twelvemile River (now named the Chandindu River) and down that to the Yukon River, from which point it is only a short haul to Dawson City. The trail in the summer was nothing more than an endless, 110-mile conglomerate of grass hummocks and swamp. In the winter, however, it was easily navigated by dog team. Dawson City had grown so spectacularly by 1907 that a telephone connection was established at a power plant built near the headwaters of Twelvemile River and about 40 miles from Dawson City. Returning patrols used this facility to call headquarters at Dawson, and often a team of horses would be sent out to assist the patrol by carrying gear and breaking trail the rest of the way in.

The other leg of the route was an age-old hunting trail from the Blackstone River across the Hart River drainage to the Wind, where it connected with the trail to Fort McPherson.

This land of the Loucheux Indians was a harsh land, and the difficulties of survival made the Loucheux Indians among the finest woodsmen on earth. Later, the men of the Lost Patrol were to die, perhaps, in part, because they did not have a Loucheux guide with them.

Chapter 6
Early Patrols

The tragic fate of the Lost Patrol was sealed by an unlikely and unrelated series of events. In order to put the Lost Patrol and the seeming inevitability of the disaster into proper perspective, we need to examine the experience of previous patrols.

Fitzgerald was called to Edmonton from Herschel Island in the summer of 1905, and he was promoted to staff sergeant in September. He returned to his post by way of Dawson City, joining the second Mountie patrol to set out for Fort McPherson from Dawson City—the only patrol to go by a different route than the others. Thus, fate took an early hand in Fitzgerald's future. If he had joined any other patrol, he probably would not have become lost 6 years later, and the tragedy would not have occurred.

The first patrol in the winter of 1904-5 had been run with Constable Harry G. Mapley of B Division of the Mounties in charge. Richard Martin served as guide, and the other members of the patrol were Stephen Bonnetplume, Jacob Njootli, an Eskimo called "Little Pete," Constables Rowley and Dever, and E. M. Bruce. The route went northeast to where it crossed the Blackstone River. Then it veered almost due east to cross to John Martin's cabin on the Hart River, and on across the Hart River divide to the Wind River. At this point, the Mounties turned north for Fort McPherson.

The patrol went smoothly. On return to Dawson City, Mapley filed a table of distances. The table, presented in Appendix A, was of considerable significance in the fate of the Lost Patrol, as will be seen later.

Mapley also led the second patrol. Although as a staff sergeant Fitzgerald outranked the constable, the fact that he

50

was en route to his duty station at Herschel Island put him in an unofficial position in relation to the patrol's command. Mapley would have consulted with him on decisions of importance. Others making the patrol that year were Constables Aubrey E. Forrest and R. H. Walker, and Indian guides Sam Smith and Louie Cardinal. A seventh man, W. Moore, was hired along the way to serve as a trailbreaker.

The route of the second patrol went southeast from Dawson City to Mayo, then almost straight north through the Wernecke Mountains and down the Wind River. Only when the men reached the confluence of the Little Wind and Wind rivers did they join the trail of the first and later patrols.

The patrol took 56 days to reach Fort McPherson—the longest of any in the entire 17-year history of the Northern trek. They were beset by weather so cold that they were unable to travel for as much as 4 days at a time. This, and the fact that the route was longer than that of the other patrols, accounted for the 8-week time period. No less than five caribou and four moose were killed along the way, with an additional 300 pounds of moose meat being purchased from Indians. In spite of this success in hunting, the patrol ran completely out of food 2 days from Fort McPherson. However, they were fortunate enough to meet some Indians near McPherson and purchased a supply of rabbits to sustain them for the rest of the trip.

Mapley wrote the patrol report. In view of the fate of the Lost Patrol under Fitzgerald, Mapley's conclusions in respect to this patrol are pertinent. The leader stated that the Mounties would have been better off without civilians along. In essence, he was saying that Indian guides were not needed.

If Mapley was of this opinion, there was a good chance that Fitzgerald by this time felt the same way, especially in view of his 1897 Klondike patrol experience with Inspector Moodie, which resulted in some dissatisfaction with Indian guides.

There were four more patrols between the time of Fitzgerald's journey with Mapley and his last, tragic patrol. Each of these four followed the original route. Their significance in relation to the Lost Patrol becomes obvious when one reads the reports.

In 1906-7, Constable Sam Carter went with the patrol because he was transferring duty stations from Dawson City to Herschel Island. The patrol commander was A. E. Forrest, who had done well on the patrol the year before. Guide for the patrol was Richard Martin, an outstanding Loucheux woodsman and hunter. The Mounties completed this patrol with few problems. They were aided at the outset by a horse and sled, which broke trail for them for the first 50 miles. This was done for most of the patrols that left from Dawson City.

It was on the basis of his journey with the 1906-7 patrol that Sam Carter told Fitzgerald several years after that he would be able to guide him from Fort McPherson to Dawson City. Because of Carter's fatal miscalculation as to the location of Forrest Creek, an important point on the route, Constable Forrest's report concerning this portion of the third patrol is relevant.

> *31st, Dec. 1906, left camp at 8:30; travelled to head of creek and crossed over the divide into a creek [later called Forrest Creek] running into the Little Wind River. These divides are very low.*

> *1st January, '07, left camp at 7:30; travelled down the creek to the Little Wind River, and down the river for about two miles and camped.*

> *2nd, left camp at 8 a.m.; continued on down the Little Wind; had a hard time on the glaciers today, the ice being so smooth and the wind so high that it was almost impossible for men and dogs to travel.*

> *3rd, left camp at 8:30; made mouth of Little Wind River, about 25 miles and camped.*

Forrest took 2 days to travel from the confluence of the creek and the Little Wind to the big Wind River. Because of the ice and wind, it is a safe assumption that the patrol did not go farther than 15 miles, and possibly less, on their first full day on the Little Wind. This means that the Forrest patrol traveled roughly 40 miles on the Little Wind River. Going by comparative estimates of distances, Carter and Fitzgerald 4 years later did not even look for the tributary of the Little Wind, which by then was called Forrest Creek, until the patrol was approximately 8 miles above it.

The most important aspect of this patrol was Sam Carter's presence. If he had not made the trip, in all likelihood Fitzgerald would have hired a Loucheux guide to show him the way in 1910-11, and tragedy would have been averted. But Sam Carter did make the trip and performed admirably in the eyes of Forrest, who complimented him and the other members of the patrol on their performance.

And fate continued to steer events toward the inevitable disaster. Hubert Darrell was employed as a trailbreaker on the patrol of 1907-8. His companions were A. E. Forrest, who had by then taken his discharge from the Mounties, Indian guide John Martin (Richard's brother), Constable A. L. Simons, and Constable W.J.D. Dempster, the patrol's commander.

Darrell was a loner in every sense of the word. He had tramped over the North Country from Fort Churchill on Hudson Bay to Herschel Island in the Beaufort Sea. He had been a trailbreaker for the Mounties along the Arctic coast. To get to Dawson City, he had walked alone, hauling a small toboggan by hand, across the mountains from Herschel Island to the Yukon River and up the river to Dawson. On that trek, he encountered the great explorer, Roald Amundsen, on the Porcupine River. Amundsen was returning to his little ship, the *Gjoa*, from Alaska after reporting his successful completion of the first voyage through the fabled Northwest Passage. Amundsen later expressed his tremendous respect for Darrell and his exploit. *"I was lost in admiration,"* wrote Amundsen. *"If you got together a few more men of his stamp, you could get to the moon."* This was high praise indeed, from the man who, a few years later, would win the race to be first to the South Pole.

Darrell performed yeoman service on the 1907-8 patrol with Dempster and Martin. He skipped a year, and then came back to make the patrol of 1909-10 as a special constable. In the summer of 1910, he went to the headwaters of the Bell River with another Mountie patrol and backpacked across the Richardson Mountains to Fort McPherson. On arriving in McPherson, Darrell was asked by the Mounties' NCO in charge, Corporal J. Somers, at Inspector Fitzgerald's request (Fitzgerald was at Herschel Island), to draw a map of the route between Fort McPherson and Dawson City. The map was not very detailed, except in relation to a branch in the trail near the Blackstone River where Darrell surmised the patrol could get into trouble. The patrol never got that far.

In the fall of 1910, Darrell showed up in an Eskimo village on Baillie Island. Typically, he was alone and dragging his worldly belongings behind him on a sled. The Eskimos invited him to stay with them for the winter, but he refused, saying he was going to his campsite near the mouth of the Anderson River. He gave the Eskimos a letter to deliver to the explorer, Stefansson, in which he said he planned to go from the Anderson River to Fort McPherson, and then over the mountains to Dawson City. He probably would have joined Fitzgerald, Carter, Kinney and Taylor on their patrol to Dawson.

But Darrell was not to go with the Mounties. He was never seen again after leaving Baillie Island. Eskimos later determined that he had reached his camp, but they were unable to unravel the mystery of his disappearance. The Northland had claimed another victim. If Darrell had joined the patrol, there is little doubt that he would have successfully guided Fitzgerald where Carter failed.

The record of each patrol provides some insight into the conditions the Mounties faced on the trail in the years prior to the disaster, and several vivid lessons. For example, two incidents during the patrol of 1908-9 point to the value of an experienced Indian guide. A. E. Forrest was accredited with being one of the most expert white trail men in the North Country, so it does him no disservice to compare him with Loucheux guide John Martin.

On January 16, 1908, with the temperature -53°F, John Martin left camp at 7 a.m. to hunt caribou along a tributary of the Little Wind River. An hour later, Forrest set out to look for game on the Wind River. The wind was so terrible on the big Wind River that Forrest could not buck it, so he returned to camp. In the meantime, Martin had climbed to the head-waters of the tributary and killed four caribou, returning shortly after Forrest. The next day the other four men retrieved the caribou, leaving Martin to rest in camp.

A week later, the lack of food was becoming critical for men and dogs because the temperature had averaged -47°F for 7 straight days. A successful hunt at this point became a necessity. On January 25, Forrest and Martin again went looking for game. The temperature at the time was -40°F. Forrest had to return to camp because his rifle froze up. Not so Martin, who succeeded in tracking down and killing five caribou by 2:30 that afternoon.

In each case, Martin effectively demonstrated what an accomplished Indian guide could do when it came to working under nearly impossible conditions. An Indian can make living in the wilderness a pleasure with a minimum of effort. Comparing an Indian to a white man is like comparing a professional with an amateur. This is not to say that white men cannot become adept at wilderness living; many have, but they also have learned much from their red brethren. The Mounties learned early the value of the Natives and used Indians as guides, interpreters and dog mushers almost from the year the North-West Mounted Police was organized in 1873. Mapley's observation after the second patrol that the Mounties should travel without Indian guides was not a wise one, its fallibility being underscored ultimately with the death of four men.

The last patrol before Fitzgerald's fatal journey was led by Constable Dempster, and included two of the four men who, with him, were to seek out and find the dead of the Lost Patrol the following year. These were Constables F. Turner and J. F. Fyfe, who were both new to the trail. The other two men on the 1909-10 patrol were Special Constables Hubert Darrell and F. Horne. This patrol went astray when Dempster decided to follow a trail that a prospector named Harry Waugh said he had broken along Caribou River. The result was that it took the men 2 days longer than usual to cross the Mountain Creek portage. Luckily, they made up the time soon afterward when they ran into a trail newly broken by Indians on the Peel River, and followed it the remaining 70 miles to Fort McPherson. This demonstrates the fact that, stamina and skill being equal, much depends upon luck in regard to making fast time on a long-distance dog-sled patrol.

Examination of reports of previous patrols across the Dawson City-Hart River-Little Wind River route gives no reason to suppose that Fitzgerald would run into logistic difficulties on his journey of 1910-11. Only the year before, Dempster and his men had met an Indian family camped on the Little Wind River. Dempster purchased 340 pounds of meat from them on the return journey from Fort McPherson. The year before that, the patrol had met a well-supplied family camped at the junction of Forrest Creek and the Little Wind River. Other patrols reported frequent signs and sightings of herds of caribou and plenty of moose throughout the region.

Indians had been commonly encountered on the Blackstone, Hart, Little Wind and Trail rivers from the beginning, and there was no reason to believe that they would not continue to be seen. Of course, there was always the chance that a lengthy cold spell could put all travelers into an arctic limbo in which neither men nor game moved any more than was absolutely necessary. Fitzgerald, from previous experience, would have been aware of such a possibility.

Chapter 7
Life on the Trail

Inspector Fitzgerald had experienced countless hours on the trail by the time he was ready to embark on his ill-fated patrol in December, 1910. Outdoor life in the Arctic appealed to him, or he would not have repeatedly requested assignments that subjected him to its rigors.

Patrol reports were brief and rarely touched on the basic emotions of a man on the trail. What were the hardships, and why did individuals like Fitzgerald, Dempster, Forrest and others continually return to face them? To better understand this life, one must take a close look at its essentials.

Day in and day out, men on the trail had to deal with sled dogs. If the dogs were not kept in good shape, an entire expedition could suffer. Dogs that were used on any long patrol had to be able to survive in temperatures that dipped to -80°F, and to pull enough of a load to make it worthwhile putting them in harness in the first place. On long patrols, the Mounties normally used five-dog teams. This number could be handled relatively easily, yet get the job done.

The sled dogs used by the Mounties were malemutes and Mackenzie River breeds. These were big animals, ranging from 80 to 150 pounds, and they often had wolf strain in them. They were willing workers and, generally speaking, of good enough nature for a driver to work them. One of their chief assets, besides stamina and ability to pull, was that their feet could stand up under snow and ice conditions better than most other breeds'. This is not to say that other dogs were not used. Labradors, for example, were found to make excellent sled dogs.

The problems involved in driving dogs mounted from the time they were slipped into harness in the morning until they were chained to a tree at night. There was never a dull moment in handling a team of canines, each member with a different personality.

The dogs were harnessed to the sled with what was called a tandem hitch; they were walked into their collars with the reins or traces on either side of them. Since most of the Mountie patrols used five-dog teams, the dogs were designated, from the sled out, as the wheel dog, then the numbers four, three, and two dogs, and, at the head, the leader. They pulled in line, one behind the other, in contrast to the fan hitch used by the Eskimos, where the dogs would each be tied to a different line and spread out fan-like in front of the sled. (This hitch was practicable on the open tundra but was impossible to use in wooded areas.)

Dogs tend to be individualists, and situations arose that sometimes resulted in injury to the musher. It was not unusual to find two dogs in one team that fought any time they came within reach of one another. Obviously, the musher had to separate them when he worked the team. However, if an accident occurred and the team became all jammed up, it was only a matter of seconds before the antagonists were at each other's throats. At such times the musher had to move quickly to break up the fight, and in doing so he exposed himself to getting a hand or leg slashed. In spite of the risk, it was imperative that he break up the fight before the dogs suffered an injury that could affect the capabilities of the entire team.

Dempster mentioned having to turn a dog out of the team for several days after its foot had been slashed in a fight. Losing the services of a dog for a few days meant the others had to work that much harder. If the dog happened to be the leader, it could mean the difference between an easy or a difficult trip.

Dogs were much the same as humans when it came to conditioning. If they had not been worked much, they had to be broken in slowly when an expedition started out. If not, they would get sick and lie down in the trail. This happened on the 1905-6 patrol with Mapley and Fitzgerald. The first day of the trip, the patrol went from Dawson City to Dominion Creek, a distance of 35 miles. The dogs were sick that evening and would not eat. Mapley admitted that they had been overworked and later wrote: *"The distance was too far the first day, although Constable Opsahl with team [horse] accompanied us, hauling the heavier part of our loads."*

Sometimes a temperamental dog would refuse to work at all, even when in good physical condition. Mulish, he would suddenly stop and refuse to budge. At such times the musher had to remove the dog from the team and let him fend for himself until he got back into the mood to work again. Once out of the team, it was not unusual for the dog to head back to his starting point. Forrest had one ornery canine leave the team and travel 170 miles back to Dawson City. Dogs that attempted a journey like this were usually killed by wolves before they got very far. Any dog suspected of being temperamental was culled from a team before a long journey was undertaken.

Contrary to what many believe, a "mean" dog was not common in a dog team if the musher could avoid it. A dog who would snap at his master was too troublesome to bother with on a long patrol. A slashed hand at -50°F could mar one's ability to shoot game, to chop wood or start a fire, and could spell the difference between life and death on the trail.

Once the team got moving, there was plenty to keep mushers like Inspector Fitzgerald busy. In those days, few toboggans had handles on them, so the musher kept the toboggan in line with a rope. Hazards were always present. Even a team pulling a heavy load could make 15 mph or more going downhill and then the driver would have to jump on

Inspector Francis J. Fitzgerald.
(*Provincial Archives of Alberta*)

Right: The reason for the Mountie post: Whalers at Herschel Island in the Beaufort Sea. The large tin building is the "bone house." (*Provincial Archives of Alberta*) Below: Fitzgerald's army contingent, the 2nd Canadian Mounted Rifles, parading through Halifax, Nova Scotia, on the way to the Boer War, March, 1900. (*Public Archives of Canada*)

Right: First Mountie unit to reach Fort McPherson in the summer of 1903. Staff Sergeant Fitzgerald is second from left. Seated is Superintendent Charles Constantine. Ironically, Constantine recommended against placing a permanent contingent of Mounties on the Arctic coast at that time. Others in the photo from left are: Constables S. S. "Moose" Munro, F. D. Sutherland, John Galpin and R. H. Walker. (*Public Archives of Canada*) Below: A bleak outpost in the Canadian Arctic, Fort McPherson, 1909. (*Glenbow Museum, Calgary*)

Constable Harry Mapley is
seated on the floor, second
from left, in this photo
taken at Dawson City in
1902. Mapley led the first
patrol between Dawson
City and Fort McPherson in
the winter of 1904-5.
(*Public Archives
of Canada*)

Right: Sergeant F. J. Fitzgerald (left) in front of one of the old sod huts at Herschel Island, about 1905. The man with him is believed to be Constable F. D. Sutherland. (*Courtesy of The Mariners Museum of Newport News, Virginia*) Below: Herschel Island, 1909. Fitzgerald spent nearly 7 years at this distant Mountie post, at the time the most northerly police post in the world. (*Provincial Archives of Alberta*)

Left: Mounties take a break for lunch on the trail along the Wind River during the 1907-8 patrol, led by Constable W.J.D. Dempster. The Indian guide at the right is John Martin. Standing at the left is Special Constable A. E. Forrest. Forrest, acknowledged to have been one of the best white trailsmen in the country, had taken his discharge from the Mounties and made an unsuccessful bid to land a mail contract over the same route. (*Public Archives of Canada*) Below: Mountie patrol prepares to leave Fort McPherson for the return to Dawson City in the spring of 1910. Commander of this patrol was Constable Dempster. The man in the center is the Reverend Charles Johnstone, a missionary who accompanied the patrol on the journey to Dawson City. (*RCMP photo*)

Patrol of 1909-10, at the outset of their grueling
journey. The members of the patrol are
F. Turner, J. F. Fyfe, H. Darrell, F. Horne and
W.J.D. Dempster. Photo was taken in front of the barracks in
Dawson City. (*Public Archives of Canada*)

74

Royal North-West Mounted Police detachment,
Dawson City, 1899. Constable Sam Carter, guide
of the Lost Patrol, is seated at right in front row.
(*Public Archives of Canada*)

Right: Return of Corporal Dempster and his party to Dawson City after finding the bodies of the men of the Lost Patrol. Note how tired the dogs are. (*RCMP photo*)
Below: Three men of the Dawson-McPherson relief patrol, spring, 1911. From left, Ex-constable F. Turner, Corporal Dempster and Constable J. F. Fyfe. (*RCMP photo*) Below right: Fitzgerald's last will, written with a chunk of charcoal on a scrap of paper at his last camp and found on his body. (*RCMP photo*)

All money in Despatch Bag
and Bank, clothes etc I leave
to my dearly beloved Mother
Mrs John Fitzgerald Halifax
God Bless all
    F. J Fitzgerald
        R. N. W. M. P.

Above: Burial ceremony for
the men of the 1910-11 patrol
at Fort McPherson. The
Reverend C. E. Whittaker is
back to camera. (*RCMP
photo*) Right: Graves of the
men of the Lost Patrol in the
churchyard at Fort
McPherson, Northwest
Territories. (*RCMP photo*)

and ride to stay with them. If the team happened to hit a sharp curve in the trail, an unwary driver could find his sled and himself snapped like a whip, and both end up flying off into space. Serious damage or injury could result if the team collided with a tree. This happened to Constable Fyfe on the patrol with Dempster in the spring of 1910, when they were traversing the Mountain Creek cutoff. He was going down a steep pitch when he lost control and the sled slammed into a tree, breaking it in half.

Heavy ice was the bane of a dog musher, and was often found where there was a continuous flow of water. The flow, such as from a spring, built up great banks of ice, called "glaciers" by the mushers. The ice might cover the side of a hill for hundreds of yards or, in areas of overflow on a creek, for several miles. Ice that was obscured by snow could result in disaster for a musher and his team if he failed to detect the ice before he was on it. More often than not in such cases—particularly if the ice was located on a hillside—the musher and his team would sprawl all over it and slide down the hill. If the area of the accident was precipitous, serious injury could result. Fitzgerald, Mapley and their companions ran into large stretches of ice on the 1905-6 patrol, which caused them considerable trouble on the trail over Braine Pass. Generally, however, after a man had been over a trail a few times, he knew where to look for ice, as it formed in the same places every year.

Another danger faced by the musher was slush ice: an experienced dog musher could look right at it and not tell it from a layer of ordinary snow. Slush ice was a thick soup made of snow, ice and water. Snow settled on it the same as it did on land, effectively disguising the wetness beneath. If the team went into it, the musher had to stop to dry his dogs' feet; if the dogs' feet were not cleared of ice, they would be cut, and a dog hobbling with a cut foot had to be let out of the team. During the 1905-6 patrol, Fitzgerald and Mapley let two footsore dogs, Ping and John, loose along the Wind River. The Mounties hoped the dogs would show up at camp that night. They never did, and wolves probably got them.

Under certain conditions, even sled dogs had to have "booties" tied over their feet to protect them from the granulated ice crystals that formed in extremely cold weather. The dogs knew these were for their own good and did not tear them off.

The most dangerous of all hazards on the trail was the chance of breaking through a snow bridge or rotten ice and falling into open water. If the water was deep, the musher and dogs were goners. Snow bridges often formed among ice jams covering open leads, and could be strong enough to hold a team. If he judged the footing to be firm, the leader would continue across the patch until the full weight of the sled came to bear on the bridge. If the leader's judgment was wrong, the entire team would suddenly break through and fall into the frigid water below. One minute the team would be there, and the next minute there would be no sign of its existence, other than a trail that ended at the broken ice.

Fitzgerald and his men always had to be ready for the reaction of their dog teams to the appearance of wildlife on the trail in front of them. On seeing a squirrel, rabbit, chickadee, moose or other active forager, a team's instinct was to take off after it like a shot from a cannon. This was another situation where a good lead dog could really prove his worth, though even a well-disciplined dog found it difficult not to bolt after a caribou or moose. If a team bolted while traveling in thick forest, there was considerable danger of the musher being thrown into a tree.

Still another way a musher could get into trouble was to let his team get away from him. The dogs were always ready to run, so the driver had to tie the sled to a tree while the dogs were being hitched up. If through some oversight the team got away, they would not stop running until the sled turned over or they became tangled up in their harness. If the trail was good, they might run for many miles before they stopped. Not only did this result in a long walk for the musher, it also could spell disaster for the team, because often the dogs would get to fighting, with serious injury the result.

Overflows and open water were hazards that Mountie

teams ran into constantly. Fitzgerald and Mapley mushed into open water in the middle of a pass on their 1905 trip. The temperature at the time was -60°F. They would have been in serious trouble but for the fact that there was a cabin only a half mile from the scene of their mishap.

Dempster mentioned mushing ankle-deep in water that covered the ice on the Little Wind River. In moderate temperatures the danger was not great. However, when the temperature was in the -50°F range, a musher had to stop immediately to build a fire and dry out.

The hazards of trail life were not only connected with mushing dogs. On the 1905 trip with Fitzgerald, Forrest's fingers froze while he dressed out a caribou he had shot shortly after the patrol left Mayo. Dempster tripped over a stick, fell against the camp stove and broke a rib during his 1910 patrol. A year later, he suffered an attack of snow blindness, caused by the glare of the sun reflected from the snow. Snow blindness subjects the sufferer to torturous pain; the eye sockets feel like they are filled with red-hot coals. John Martin was doing a regular camp chore when he was hurt on one of the patrols. He cut down a tree, which split and fell back, hitting him in the head and knocking him senseless.

These were some of the hazards of life on the trail. Most of the problems could be avoided by the man who paid attention to his business. An accident that was minor in moderate weather could have very serious consequences at extremely low temperatures. When the temperatures were -50° to -60°F, death was a constant companion of the careless or unlucky.

The great dread on the trail was frostbite. Frostbite, with rare exceptions, is limited to the body's extremities—hands, feet, nose, ears, chin and cheeks. The first visual evidence of frostbite is that exposed skin will turn white. A light case will result in numbness to the frostbitten area, followed by its turning blue or mottled. The affected skin will swell, sting and burn for some time. Deep frostbite is far worse, resulting in the formation of huge blisters that take from 3 days to a week to develop. Swelling of an entire hand or foot will take place and may last for a month or more after the victim has been brought in from the cold. While this is happening, the victim is extremely limited in his use of the injured extremity, which will turn blue, violet or gray. Aching, throbbing and shooting pains may last for as long as 2 months. Under treatment, the blisters will finally dry up, turn black and slough off. This leaves only the delicate underlayer of the skin covering the affected part, which will take months to toughen and return to normal, and often will remain permanently sensitive to the cold.

The biggest problem with frostbite is that it can so incapacitate a man that he cannot perform normal tasks needed to warm his entire body, with the result that a condition called *hypothermia* sets in. This is the loss of body heat—a lowering of the temperature of the body's inner core. In an acute case, it can result in uncontrollable shivering, followed by increasing clumsiness, loss of judgment, thickness of speech, dilation of the pupils, stupor, and finally unconsciousness and death.

The trailsman must be on the lookout for a number of conditions that can cause heat loss. These include cold, wet, wind and the personal state of the traveler. If he is exhausted, sick, injured or starving, death through heat loss can easily occur. Heat is produced by shivering, physical exercise, diseases that cause fever and the basal metabolic rate that produces heat from food and oxygen intake. There are, therefore, a number of ways of increasing body heat. An effective way is exercise. A short period of exercise can increase body heat production up to 10 times as much as the basal rate. Another method is through external sources, such as building a fire, drinking hot liquids, and absorption from other bodies or sunlight.

The areas on the body most vulnerable to loss of heat are the head and neck. An unprotected head may cause a person to lose up to *one-half* of a body's total heat production at 40°F, and up to *three-quarters* of the total at 5°F.

Failure to wear properly insulated clothing aids in heat loss. This can be accentuated by wind; a person can die quickly in a surprisingly warm temperature if he is not wearing a windbreaker. (See Appendix B for this "wind chill" factor.)

Immersion can also be a killer: falling into 30°F water can be fatal due to hypothermia in as little as a minute and a half.

After years on the trail, a man like Inspector Fitzgerald would certainly have been aware of the signs of heat loss in a companion. He himself would have felt and been aware of the symptoms at various times: intense shivering and fatigue, feeling of deep cold or numbness, poor coordination, blueness or puffiness of the skin, decrease in shivering and a slow pulse rate.

The man on the trail had to be vigilant for these signs and note them immediately. Constable Walker, who was on the patrol of 1905-6 with Mapley and Fitzgerald, complained at one point that he could not go on after traveling an hour with the temperature at -51°F and a 25 mph wind blowing. In defense of Walker, it is small wonder that he was cold, because the wind-chill factor would have been -120°F! Fires had to be made and tea brewed almost hourly at such temperatures; a man on the trail should not wait until he is cold or exhausted before starting a fire or making camp. But most Mountie patrol leaders expected their men to take the cold without complaint until the leaders decided conditions were beyond endurance.

The principal requirement at low temperatures is food to create energy and heat, which is expended maintaining normal body temperature. The lower the outside temperature, the more food—especially food of high fat content—is needed to "stoke the furnace." For example, when the outside temperature is -60°F, it is -158°F lower than that of a human being, whose normal temperature is 98.6°F. There is no room for malfunction. If this chain breaks down and the fuel is not available, the extremities of a person's body begin to freeze, even though covered with adequate clothing.

The Mounties were usually careful about their supplies when they traveled on the Dawson City-Fort McPherson route. Food with a high fat content was a *must* item. The patrols figured on 30 days of supplies, based on a daily average distance of about 15 miles. If the Mounties went over this 30-day estimate, they were then dependent on what additional food they could acquire along the way. For this reason they shot game whenever they had the chance and often purchased food for themselves and their dogs from Indians along the way. Food commonly used by both dogs and men included caribou, moose and bacon. Dried fish was a staple supplied to the dogs, but could also be eaten by the men in emergencies.

Seemingly, these problems and dangers would be enough to discourage any person from actively seeking exposure to them. But Fitzgerald kept going "back to the well" until it finally engulfed him. Why did he choose to lead the patrol of 1910-11, particularly when he was so close to retirement? It may have been that service on Herschel Island had become so boring that anything would have been better than remaining there for another long winter. Or it may have been simply that he liked the life on the trail. He left us no explanation.

What was there about the life that drew men to it? Was it a Circe-like allure? When asked, those who have lived it may put it differently, but in each case they give witness to an extreme *sense of being* on the trail; all of the senses of sight, smell, touch, taste and hearing are acutely brought into play. This is combined with a puzzling and bewitching mystique which hovers over the vast expanse of tundra and wilderness, especially in winter. The overwhelming silence that envelops the Northern forest in winter makes the contrast of sight and sound that much more stark. The dangers of the life are secondary to the lure that constantly beckons them back.

But the dangers, too, are a part of it. Man's adventures and misadventures have contributed to the mystique of the North. Men by the score have disappeared from the face of the earth, leaving no clues as to the cause of their disappearance. To some others, this adds spice to the life and enhances their own sense of adventure.

There are oddities that sometimes make up a part of this mystique. One graphic tale was told the author by Jack MacKenzie, the man who drove the last mail sled on the upper Yukon River. He had spent years on the trail driving the mail, and other years alone as a trapper. Because the arctic night is so long, he passed innumerable hours looking at the night sky with its dazzling displays of northern lights, its myriad flickering stars and brilliant arctic moon. There was more, the trapper said. There were black lights. They were to him like deep black holes in the sky. They were not clouds: he would see black lights only when the nights were clear. He could think of no reason for their being, other than that he had seen them.

The same man contended that he had never *heard* the northern lights, a comment that can always generate controversy in the North Country. Some claim they have heard a static sound accompanying the northern lights at rare intervals. Scientists tell us that this is impossible, but is anything really impossible in the ethereal North?

Legend becomes immersed in fact and fills men with wonder. Tales of strange creatures, often half human, half ape, that roam the Northern forests permeate every stretch of the Arctic and sub-Arctic from sea to sea.

The magnetism of trail life in the North is made up of many things. It is the crack of a spruce tree splitting in the frigid temperature. It is the flickering of candlelight that cheerily illuminates a canvas shelter. It is the startling flutter of wings when a flock of ptarmigan rise from an approaching dog team. It is the silent dance of the multicolored aurora as it flits across the skies. It is the physical exhilaration of meeting each day's challenge and mastering it. It is the wholesome smell of caribou steak sizzling in a frying pan and setting the saliva to flow. It is the crunch of snowshoes and the rasp of a toboggan as it grates across an ice hummock. It is the comic gurgle of the raven as he hops into camp looking for a handout. It is the sibilant sound of ice expanding and contracting on a nearby creek. It is the fragrant aroma of spruce boughs that permeates the tent at night. It is the sight of a band of caribou wandering specter-like in the morning mists. It is the camaraderie of men helping one another to achieve a common goal. It is the refreshing freedom of the trail.

Chapter 8
The Fatal Patrol

December 21, 1910, four men with three dog teams stood in front of the Hudson's Bay trading post at Fort McPherson, exchanging quips with those waiting to see them off. A strong north wind swirled pea-soup mist up the Peel River. The temperature was -21°F. What light there was showed the day to be cold, gray and dismal.

The four men and their dog teams comprised the seventh Royal North-West Mounted Police patrol to be undertaken between Dawson City and Fort McPherson, and the first of the patrols to have Fort McPherson as the starting point.* The distance to Dawson City was 475 miles. Broken into segments, it was 70 miles up the Peel to Trail River, 81 miles along the east flank of the Richardson Mountains to cut off the great bend of the Peel, 10 miles along the Peel to the mouth of the Wind River, 49 miles up that river to the Little Wind River and about 40 miles up the Little Wind to Forrest Creek. From there the route ran west and southwest to Dawson City.

Inspector Francis J. "Frank" Fitzgerald shook hands with Corporal Somers of the McPherson post and waved goodbye to John Firth and other Hudson's Bay men and Indians standing by. The cry "Mush!" was heard, and the 4 men and 15 dogs lurched forward on a journey from which they would never return.

The men accompanying Fitzgerald were former Constable Sam Carter (the guide) and Constables George Frances Kinney and Richard O'Hara Taylor. Sam Carter had recently

---

*It would be more correct to say that the actual starting point was Herschel Island since that was where Fitzgerald was, but he did not write a log for the initial leg from Herschel to Fort McPherson.

retired from the Mounties after 21 years of service and married an Eskimo girl. He had originally joined the North-West Mounted Police on April 28, 1888, about 7 months before Fitzgerald. Carter had served at Regina, Battleford, Prince Albert and Dawson City before going to Fort McPherson and Herschel Island.

Kinney was an American. His parents had died when he was quite young, and he was raised by an uncle and aunt in Chicago. At the age of 17, he fought with the U.S. Army during the Spanish-American War. After combat experience in Cuba, he volunteered for service in the Philippines, where he spent 4 years in the infantry. At the end of that time, he returned to the United States and worked on ranches in the west. Kinney then joined the Royal North-West Mounted Police on May 3, 1907, and served at Regina before going North.

Taylor had joined the Mounties on March 18, 1905, and was posted to Fort McPherson in May, 1910. Taylor had been born in Scotland, and for a short while lived with his father in Australia. Before joining the Mounties, he sailed as second officer on one of the ships of the White Star Line. At the time of the patrol, Taylor was 28 and Kinney was 27. Fitzgerald and Carter were both 41.

The primary purpose of the patrol was the same as in previous years—to carry mail and dispatches between the Arctic posts at Herschel and Fort McPherson and Dawson City in the south. Another, minor purpose of the patrol was to check on the condition of Indians and prospectors who were wandering through the north-central Yukon Territory. Of the six previous patrols, five of them had been over the route Fitzgerald's party would follow.

The Mounties were equipped with the usual trail clothes worn on such expeditions. These included long woolen underwear, dungarees or regular issue pants, wool shirts and a duck parka with a fur-lined hood. The parka extended to the knees, fitted loosely over the layers of woolen clothes underneath and served as a windbreaker. Wool is warm, but it must have a finer, tighter-woven material over it to hold the heat generated by the body, particularly when there is a strong wind. Wool hats or toques were worn. Wool socks were brought along in profusion, as were fur-lined mittens, Indian moccasins and several pairs of mukluks for each man.

They also took along down-filled Alaska sleeping bags, a Yukon stove, a tent, and tarps to wrap the gear lashed on their three 10-foot birchwood toboggans.

Total weight of provisions placed aboard the sleds was 1,302 pounds, or 434 pounds per sled. Nine hundred pounds of this was dried fish for the dogs, and there were also 18 pounds of candles and 28 pounds of tobacco, leaving a balance of 89 pounds of food for each man. Weight of camping and personal gear, including cooking utensils, a .30-30 carbine, two axes, a pocket barometer, watches and matches, brought the total weight per sled to around 600 pounds.

Taking a more detailed look at provisions, the total amount of meat loaded aboard the sleds (other than fish) was 75 pounds of bacon and 10 pounds of corned beef. It is interesting to note that the 28 pounds of tobacco equalled about one third of the total amount of meat brought along. They also carried 15 pounds of lard, 3 pounds of salt, 10 pounds of butter, 20 pounds of milk in tins, 120 pounds of flour, 15 pounds of dried fruit, 30 pounds of beans, 17 pounds of coffee and tea, 6 pounds of baking powder, and 35 pounds of sugar.

The men set out up the Peel River. Since there were three dog teams and four men, one man could always be breaking trail ahead of the dogs. That first day the trail turned out to be quite heavy from recent snows—much heavier than Fitzgerald would have liked so early in the trip. With an even break on luck they would have had some kind of a broken trail to follow on at least the first 70-mile leg of the trip, but as it turned out, no trappers or hunters had preceded them up the Peel. In this, it was not like leaving from the other end of the route at Dawson City, where a horse and sled was often employed to break trail for the first 50 miles. This gave dogs and men a good chance to get their "trail legs" before they engaged in the heavier work of traveling an unbroken trail. Fitzgerald was aware of this situation, and it is doubtful that he planned to try to break any speed records between the two towns.

The patrol made 15 miles the first day and stayed that night in a vacant cabin. The next day the wind switched to the south, which meant that they now had to buck it. The mists held on and made it difficult to see. However, the trail was firmer than the first day, allowing easier travel. They traveled 18 miles, and camped that night in a tent.

The ritual for setting up a tent camp when mushing dogs has varied little over the centuries. The first task is to unharness the dogs and chain them to trees far enough apart so that the radii allowed by their chains does not overlap. This keeps them from fighting over food or anything else that happens to come into their minds. The men then cut poles for the tent, strip spruce boughs for the floor of the tent, cut and trim two logs on which the stove is placed and chop enough wood to last through the night.

Other chores to be done include checking the dogs' feet to make sure they are in good shape, turning over and scraping ice from toboggans, repairing snowshoes that may have been damaged during the day, chopping ice to melt on the stove for water, cooking, washing up, feeding the dogs and hanging wet gear up to dry on a line strung inside the tent. On the first night out, each man picks a place in the tent to bed down, and he usually sleeps in the same spot every night for the rest of the trip.

In the morning, the procedure is reversed in breaking camp. Utensils are washed, gear packed, tent folded and dogs hitched up—all tasks usually done in frigid temperatures.

On December 23 it snowed, making the trail heavy, but the

patrol still managed to mush 17 miles. It continued to snow that night, with the result that the trail was even heavier on Christmas Eve. Nevertheless, they traveled 16 more miles.

Christmas Day the temperature dropped to -30°F, with a light northwest wind and a heavy mist. Fitzgerald and his men reached Trail River at 10 a.m. and retrieved a cache of fish that had been placed there earlier. They veered away from the Peel River at this point to traverse the cutoff, and picked up a fresh trail broken through the snow by a party of Indians. This made the going easier, and they made 16 miles, despite the time lost loading up from the fish cache. They had now completed the first leg of the trip in good condition, though the going had not been easy.

The day after Christmas, they mushed up Trail River for 18 miles. The Mounties were again plagued by mist. They had to beat into a strong southeast wind all day, but the packed trail made it much easier for the men and the dogs. They made camp with several Indian families shortly after noon at the foot of Caribou Born Mountain, one of the two mountains they would have to cross on the portage. They found out from the Indians that their packed trail was not the main one over the cutoff, which they had missed, so Fitzgerald hired Esau George to break trail and guide them across the portage to the Peel River. (When he first arrived at Dawson City, Esau reported that the Mounties had been lost at this point, and his comments were partly responsible for the decision to send out Dempster's search patrol.)

With hindsight, it would appear that here the inspector should either have hired Esau to take them all the way through to Dawson City or turned back. Fitzgerald and Carter had both been over the cutoff before. In view of the fact that they could not find their way over this part of the trail, so close to Fort McPherson, Fitzgerald was assuming a high risk in depending on Sam Carter to lead them across the 300 remaining miles of a trail that he had traveled but once, and in the opposite direction.

On December 27, with Esau leading and breaking trail through unusually deep snow, they traveled 12 miles.

The temperature dropped to -43°F on December 28. The party ascended a ravine and eventually camped on the north slope of Caribou Born Mountain. The Indian families followed the patrol and camped with them again that night. Fitzgerald estimated they had climbed a thousand feet in making good another 12 miles. They were now 1,800 feet above the Trail River.

The next day the patrol traveled 14 miles. Fitzgerald noted that the excruciating work involved in crossing the deep snow of the portage made the dogs extremely tired.

On December 30, the temperature plummeted to -51°F, limiting the day's travel to 9 miles. The next day the Mounties mushed 16 miles, and on New Year's Day 11 miles to reach a cabin on Mountain Creek, 4 miles from the Peel River. Here, Esau was paid a total of $24 for guiding them for 5 days and for another 3 days for his return trip. The party reached the Peel again on the morning of January 2. It had taken them 8 days to traverse the 80-mile portage. The average mileage per day was no worse than some of the other patrols, but based on Fitzgerald's estimates, they actually traveled 101 miles, a longer distance than previous patrols over this section.

They had now completed the second leg of the trip. They had been on the trail for 12 full days, and had gone 150 miles. This left them 18 days to complete the journey, based on their 30-day allotment of supplies. Since they were averaging 12 miles a day, this meant they would take 9 days more than the 30 days they had estimated for the trip. However, the portage was the most difficult part of the journey, and there was no reason for Fitzgerald to believe that they would not make better time now that that was behind them. Unfortunately, on this patrol good luck was taking a holiday.

The Mounties were now battered by a brutal cold snap which saw the *average* temperature for the next 7 days hit a bone-chilling -51°F. As if that was not enough, deep snow, open water and huge piles of driftwood on the ice of the river made the going still more difficult. It took Fitzgerald and his men 7 days to go the next 70 miles.

The first day back on the Peel they were hit by a heavy

snowstorm. Piles of driftwood forced them off the river, and they had to cut their way through thick brush on the river banks, limiting their distance to 10 miles. On January 3, the temperature stood at -46°F as they worked their way 10 miles up the Peel River to the Wind, and then 2 miles up the Wind to camp at prospector Harry Waugh's abandoned tent. The trail was extremely heavy, and Fitzgerald commented that the dogs were just about played out.

A strong southeast wind greeted the patrol the next day. The temperature was -47°F, and 3 feet of billowing snow made the going rough. The Mounties mushed up the Wind River past Wind City, where so many men had died of scurvy in the gold rush of 1898. They camped that night only a few miles above Wind City, after making only 10 miles. Their average distance should have been improving, but it was getting worse.

The cold smothered them the next day when the mercury dropped to -65°F. Traveling at such a low temperature is an experience men do not look back on with nostalgia. In such conditions, the moisture from a man's breath condenses on his face and freezes to form thin sheets of ice on his eyelids, cheeks, nose and around his mouth and chin. The chill goes right through a man, and just to walk becomes an effort. Material becomes brittle. A man can split a 24-inch log with one easy tap of an ax. Snowshoes can snap if medium pressure is put on them. Ax handles break easily, and even the steel head can shatter. According to Charley River, who made the trip in 1914, mists hang so thick from the breath of men and dogs that the man driving the last team cannot see the first team in line. Fitzgerald's patrol made 6 miles, and suffered slight frostbite. More days like this and he would have to consider aborting the trip.

January 6, the mercury climbed to -54°F, but that did not mean it was actually warmer, as Fitzgerald noted there was a very strong headwind. If we assume that he meant the wind was difficult to walk against, that would place the velocity between 10 and 20 mph, and the wind-chill factor at around -110°F. The Mounties camped that night on the downstream side of Mount Deception. Heavy snow had again slowed their progress, yet they still made 11 miles. Considering the conditions, it was a superhuman effort.

As on so many previous patrols, open water from warm springs in that area caused the patrol to make a number of detours the next day, their 18th on the trail. The going was slightly better, but they only covered 13 miles. The temperature was -51°F when they made camp that night about 6 miles below the confluence of the Wind and Little Wind rivers.

The cold spell continued to pummel the patrol yet another day. On January 8, a Sunday, the temperature sank to -64°F, with a strong headwind. They camped early, 3 miles up the Little Wind River, after trudging 9 miserable miles.

Mother Nature smiled down on the severely buffeted patrol on January 9. The temperature warmed up to a pleasant -22°F. If Fitzgerald had any thoughts of turning back, it would have been the day before. They had been struggling for 19 days and had gone less than halfway to their destination. They had only enough food for 11 more days. The temperatures had been extremely cold. This, then, was the day they were looking for to make up for those days when they had made little distance. The lay of the land was better now, too; they had passed the worst of the patches of open water on the Wind River. There was a heavy timber belt at the mouth of the Little Wind, and the river itself was broken up by numerous willow-covered islands and gravel bars. The timber belt extended up the Little Wind valley. Moose and caribou were often spotted on the Little Wind, and the patrol was 3 or 4 days from crossing over to the usually prolific game country of the Hart River.

Little did Fitzgerald and his men realize that the warm weather was a treacherously false promise of better things to come. The warmth, combined with easier travel on the Little Wind River, made a pleasant day for them on the 9th. They traveled 16 miles, which was as good a day as they had had on the trip, and made camp at 3 p.m. They were now about 20 miles up the Little Wind River, and there was no apparent reason not to continue the patrol.

The good weather held on January 10, but a stiff wind kept blowing the dogs off their feet on clear ice. They made 15 miles and camped that night about 35 miles up the Little Wind River.

Warm weather continued to stay with them the next day, but it was a mixed blessing. The entire river was in overflow when they awoke in the morning, and as a result, they were able to go only 9 miles. The men suffered from wet feet, which made the day's journey an unpleasant one. They pitched camp at 3:30 p.m., 44 miles up the river. They were near Forrest Creek, but did not look for the creek here.

On January 12, the Mounties took to the trail at 8 a.m. and during a 3-hour lunch stop, Fitzgerald sent Carter out to look for Forrest Creek. They were now at least 8 miles past the creek, and Carter could not find the trail. Fitzgerald debated whether to go on or go back, and finally decided to keep going forward. His decision sealed the fate of the patrol. They went on until the stream of the Little Wind got so small Fitzgerald knew they had missed Forrest Creek. They made camp at 3 p.m. and were now, according to Inspector Fitzgerald's calculations, 56 miles up the Little Wind River. Carter elected to take a look farther up the river, but saw nothing that looked familiar. Their supplies had dwindled to 9 days' reserves. This was still enough to reach Dawson City, though they would be pressed if they did not shoot any game along the way.

Fitzgerald and his men now started marching up and down the Little Wind River and its tributaries like Caesar rampaging through Gaul, searching for the Forrest Creek trail.

Friday, January 13, proved as unlucky as it is supposed to be. The weather held at a warm -12°F. The patrol broke camp and anxiously proceeded to backtrack for 5 miles until they turned up a small stream that Carter thought was Forrest Creek. They followed this for 4 miles and found it to be the wrong one. They came back down that creek and then went 2 miles farther down the Little Wind River. The patrol traveled 15 miles total, though they had actually only moved down the Little Wind a total of 7 miles above Forrest Creek. They

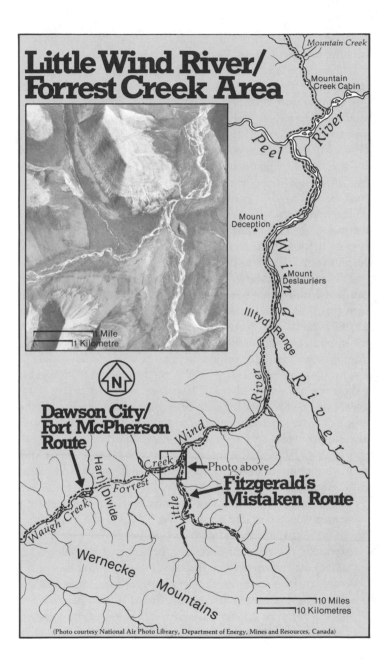

Little Wind River/ Forrest Creek Area

Mountain Creek

Mountain Creek Cabin

Peel River

Mount Deception

Mount Deslauriers

Illtyd Range

Wind River

1 Mile
1 Kilometre

Dawson City/ Fort McPherson Route

Wind

Creek

Forrest

Hart Divide

Waugh Creek

Little

Photo above

Fitzgerald's Mistaken Route

Wernecke

Mountains

10 Miles
10 Kilometres

(Photo courtesy National Air Photo Library, Department of Energy, Mines and Resources, Canada) camped at 1:30 p.m., and Fitzgerald again sent Carter out looking for the portage. Carter had no luck.

Though the weather was still warm, a gale kept the patrol in camp on the 14th. Their course the next day is an enigma. The temperature dropped to -39°F and the men encountered a slight headwind as they continued their search. Fitzgerald wrote in his diary: ". . . *followed up east branch of Little Wind River and camped at 3:15 p.m. at what is supposed to be the mouth of Forrest Creek. Going very good; a little heavy snow at the start; the rest of the way mostly ice. Sixteen miles.*"

The question arises as to what stream Fitzgerald was referring as the east branch of the Little Wind River. Whatever it was, it took them 16 miles in the wrong direction, and the 16 miles would have to be retraced on the way back.

The temperature was -43°F the next day, when the patrol mushed 6 miles up a tributary of the "east branch" to find out that this, too, was the wrong creek. They traveled a total of 12 miles and ended up where they had started from that morning. The exhausted party had now been out for 26 days and possessed food for only 4 days more at a normal ration.

The weather warmed to -23°F on January 17. However, gale-force winds hit them. Desperate now, Inspector Fitzgerald decided to send his men in all directions looking for the creek. Carter and Kinney followed one watercourse south and slightly east, only to find that it ran right up against high mountains. Fitzgerald himself followed a river running due south but could not see any ax cuttings that would indicate a trail. Fitzgerald wrote in his diary:

> We have now only ten pounds of flour and eight pounds of bacon and some dried fish. My last hope is gone, and the only thing I can do is return, and kill some of the dogs to feed the others and ourselves, unless we can meet some Indians. We have now been a week looking for a river to take us over the divide, but there are dozens of rivers and I am at a loss. I should not have taken Carter's word that he knew the way from the Little Wind River.

So Inspector Fitzgerald realized finally that they would have to turn back to Fort McPherson. The patrol had spent 9 days and wandered 98 miles on the Little Wind River when a patrol normally spent about 2 days to go the correct 40 miles.

Why had Sam Carter missed the trail? The reason could have been simply that Carter was so preoccupied with the extensive overflow of water they encountered on the river when they reached the mouth of Forrest Creek that he missed the turnoff. In fact, the overflow may very well have come from Forrest Creek. Evidently, Carter had forgotten both the distance and the amount of time it had taken his party 4 years earlier to descend the Little Wind below Forrest Creek.

Chapter 9
Death on the Trail

The patrol started back to Fort McPherson on January 18. The Mounties made good time, as the moderate temperature held for another day, and they covered 20 miles. That night, they killed the first dog to feed those remaining in the team, but hardly any of the dogs would touch the meat. The men each ate a small piece of bannock and some dried fish.

The need for killing a dog so soon is graphic evidence that Fitzgerald waited woefully long before deciding to turn back. Even then, should it have been killed so early? Should Fitzgerald instead have fed the fish to the dogs and kept the men on starvation rations as long as possible before killing dogs? Should he have pushed the dogs to the limit of their endurance before killing them? In this situation the patrol was faced with a dilemma: Do you feed the dogs, or do you feed yourself? The dogs are your lifeline, but you must also have the strength to handle them. Who can go farther without food, dog or man? It was a fine balance upon which the lives of the men depended.

The next day was again a good one for travel. Fitzgerald reported they mushed 21 miles and camped for the night about 29 miles upstream from the Wind River. They killed a second dog that day to feed the others, who did not this time refuse the meat. The patrol had now covered 41 miles in 2 days. If moderate weather conditions had persisted and their back trail had held up, they could probably have made it back to Fort McPherson without misfortune.

But the weather began to worsen on January 20. With the temperature at -21°F, a gale blew up and it was all they could do to keep the tent from blowing away. This bit of bad luck was the first of many such setbacks they would experience on the rugged journey toward home. Every hour's delay meant that an hour's energy was being lost from virtually unfueled bodies, accelerating the deterioration of the men. That day they ate the last of their flour and bacon.

The gale continued through noon the next day, but they broke camp anyway at 7 a.m. Although the temperature was comparatively mild at 0°F, the chill factor with gale-force winds would have been around -50°F. Fitzgerald knew that they could not delay their travel any longer, even though conditions were bad. They made camp that night 12 miles from the Wind River and killed another dog, leaving 12 to pull them through to McPherson. Despite the fact that the dogs had been living on sparse rations, to Fitzgerald they seemed in good enough condition to haul the men all the way, given reasonable weather. But for men and dogs alike, any change for the worse could tip the scales. They were now living only on a little dried fish, dog meat and tea. If the temperatures dropped considerably, they would be in dire straits, and this is just what happened.

On Sunday, January 22, the temperature fell from 0° to -50°F in less than 4 hours, and then plummeted to -64°F that afternoon. It was as if a giant blanket had been cast over the entire region, rendering every being virtually helpless. Yet the men persevered through these terrible conditions to travel 17 miles. They reached the main Wind River and camped that night 5 miles below the mouth of the Little Wind. Nature now worked overtime against the patrol. The gale that had plagued the patrol 2 days earlier had swept through the length and breadth of the region, with the result that the Mounties' back trail, which had been so strenuously broken, was now filled in again. In some winters a back trail might hold up several weeks or even a month, but it was not to be this winter.

Strong headwinds with -64°F temperatures kept the men in camp on Monday, the 23rd, again causing valuable time to be lost in what was turning into a race against death. Heavy mist made visibility almost nil. They had been on the trail 33 days.

The next day dawned bleak and bitterly cold again, and the strong winds continued. Fitzgerald had no choice but to try to make a few miles. The temperature was -56°F when the men set out. The patrol struggled 6 miles down the Wind River, only to find it open all the way across. They then had to climb the riverbank to by-pass the open stretch, and in doing this, Taylor went into the water up to his waist and Carter up to his hips. Camp was quickly made to thaw out the two men, and they killed and ate another dog. Total gain for the day was only 6 miles.

The following afternoon they found part of their old trail while skirting the open water. They "nooned" 3 miles above Mount Deception. Fitzgerald estimated they had gone 18 miles that day, making camp 20 miles from the Peel River. They killed a dog and drank some tea. This was the sole extent of their rations. The raw cold continued to batter them, with the temperature hovering at -53°F.

Warmer weather greeted the patrol on January 26, but the deck remained stacked against them. The warmer weather brought new snow. The party lost 3 hours tramping through the heavy snow getting around open water, and Fitzgerald remarked in his diary that both men and dogs were growing noticeably weaker. They made only 8 miles, with the temperature at -21°F.

On Friday, January 27, the snowstorm continued. The patrol spent 5½ hours on the trail, plus an hour break at noon. They reached prospector Harry Waugh's tent, passed on the trek south, and camped. The hungry men searched his tent and cache hopefully for food but found none and had to kill another dog, leaving them nine. Fitzgerald estimated that they covered 11 miles that day.

Taylor was sick all the next day, nevertheless the patrol continued on. They made 12 miles and pitched their tent in one of their old camps on the Peel River. They plunged on the next day, their 40th on the trail, to reach the cabin 4 miles up Mountain Creek. They killed another dog here. The temperature was -20°F, with a slight northeast wind. They cached one toboggan, a tarp and seven dog harnesses at the cabin.

Fitzgerald and his men were now back on the Mountain Creek cutoff. They had 80 miles to go before they would again reach the Peel River, and 150 to Fort McPherson. Unfortunately, the 80 miles were the ruggedest section of the entire route between Fort McPherson and Dawson City; they would have to cross two mountains. The snow was even deeper now, and their old trail was covered. It had taken them 8 days to cross the portage when they were in good health and had a full complement of dogs. Fitzgerald probably realized at this point that their chances of making it back alive were rapidly fading, but there was always hope. They might run into the Indians they had met earlier, or perhaps a trapper could be found wandering through the country who could supply enough food to keep them going.

The next morning the temperature warmed up to an inviting -20°F. Fitzgerald decided to press on. However, only a few hours out on the trail the temperature dropped to -51°F and remained in this range as they forced themselves up Mountain Creek to cross the big hill at its head. They ate more dog meat, becoming sick on the liver, and they retched continually as they staggered up the trail. The raw cold nipped at their cheekbones, creating white patches of frostbite on skin stretched tightly over their gaunt faces. The men were now probably walking as if in the initial stage of drunkenness. The desire to lie down and go to sleep is compelling for an exhausted man, but to do this means death under such conditions, and men must urge each other on. It was now more a matter of steps than miles for the Mounties. Each step was a physical obstacle to be undertaken and overcome all on its own. In this manner, they fought their way up Mountain Creek through the heavy snow.

The temperature plunged to -62°F on the evening of January 31. The dogs were now pulling two sleds, with four dogs on each sled. To climb the slope, the men had to hitch the two teams together and pull the sleds one at a time up the steep incline. The agony of the physical effort of breaking trail and pushing and tugging to help the dogs pull the sleds up the hill must have been excruciating to men consumed by sickness and exhaustion. The physical effects of living on nothing but dog meat began to show. Their skin started peeling off and their lips swelled and split open, indicating frostbite and possibly scurvy.

The patrol continued up and over the Mountain Creek hill and down to the Caribou River, then up that to Caribou Born Mountain. The temperature was -51°F on February 1 when the men found part of their old trail, but snow had drifted across it, making the going heavy. The eighth dog was killed, leaving seven for the two sleds. The next day the temperature sky-rocketed to 7°F. Heavy mist clung to the mountain as the men plowed through waist-deep snow. Fearing that they might lose their way, they finally made camp to await better visibility.

They crossed Caribou Born Mountain on February 3 and reached Trail River, having now managed to surmount the worst obstacles of the trip. The ninth dog was killed to feed the remaining few. This was the 45th day of their epic journey, and they had 100 miles to go. Fitzgerald now was optimistic about their chances, figuring they would reach McPherson and still have three or four dogs left. His main concern was the weather. The temperature on that day was a relatively mild -26°F. If the mercury remained as mild, they might make it. If there was ever a time in the trip when they needed a break in the weather, it was now. They did not get it.

The next day the temperature dropped to -52°F as the men endeavored to make their way down the Trail River. The frigid arctic air engulfed the Mounties as they labored to stand up under the will-shattering effects of the bitter cold. After spending another night, men and dogs staggered wearily down the Trail River to the Peel, which they reached on February 5. They covered only 8 miles that day, and in the process Inspector Fitzgerald broke through the ice. He floundered ashore and made a fire, but was not quick enough to avoid freezing one foot. The temperature was -48°F. Later, still another dog was killed, leaving five dogs. Fitzgerald noted that the men's skin continued to peel off as the effects of frostbite, starvation and scurvy took their toll.

Inspector Fitzgerald's diary ended on Saturday, February 5. The men were roughly 70 miles from their goal. They could have covered the distance in 4 days under normal conditions. Even in their poor state, with a good trail and moderate weather, they might have made it in a week. In his last entry, Fitzgerald recorded that they could *only go a few miles a day.* It is likely that temperatures continued in the -50° to -60°F range during the following week.

The men of the Lost Patrol reeled down the Peel River the next day.

The rest of the picture must be put together by Corporal Dempster's discoveries, and later observations made by Corporal Somers.

Superintendent Snyder, in command at Dawson City, had interviewed the Indian, Esau, and others in his party on February 20, the day they arrived in Dawson. Their report that they had met Fitzgerald on the Trail River as long ago as December 26—and that he had missed the regular route— added considerably to Snyder's already growing concern. Snyder tried to wire his superior, Commissioner A. Bowen Perry in Regina, on February 20 to request permission to send a relief patrol in search of the overdue men. The Canadian telegraph line was down at this time, however, so Snyder had to send his wire by way of the U.S. telegraph line. The same day, he ordered Dempster to Dawson City from his regular post at Forty Mile. But another full week was to be lost. Because of the re-routing of the message, he did not receive authorization from Regina to send Dempster out until February 27.

On February 28, Corporal W.J.D. Dempster, Constable J. F. Fyfe, ex-Constable F. Turner and Indian guide Charles Stewart set out on the first leg of their now-historic patrol to search for Fitzgerald and his men.

Dempster was plagued by overflows and ice while traveling over Seela Pass to the Blackstone River. Temperatures during this time averaged -35°F, with strong winds bringing the chill factor down to the -80°F mark. Turner's feet were frostbitten the third day of the trip, and he was to suffer considerably for the next 10 days as a result.

By March 7, the Dempster patrol had reached John Martin's cabin on the Hart River, a regular stopping place for the patrols. The corporal pondered Fitzgerald's fate. He thought it likely that Inspector Fitzgerald and his men had encountered some sort of trouble and had returned to Fort McPherson. Dempster could not visualize anything worse happening to a man as experienced as Fitzgerald. A "Northern" in the truest sense, it seemed highly unlikely that Fitzgerald could be in any desperate trouble. However, Dempster was also well aware that in a region with as fickle a climate as the Arctic, nothing could be taken for granted, so he pressed on in a race that was already lost.

It took his patrol 5 more days to find the first trace of Fitzgerald's trail, on the Little Wind River. On March 12, Dempster found traces of an old trail on the river but was not sure if it had been made by Inspector Fitzgerald's patrol or by Indians. Later that day, Dempster reached and went up the Wind River until he determined that Fitzgerald had not continued up that river by mistake. He then proceeded down the Wind below its junction with the Little Wind and late the same day found one of Inspector Fitzgerald's old camps. March 13, he passed another of the inspector's camps about 4 miles distant from the one discovered the previous day. On March 14, he picked up the trail a few times and passed three more of Fitzgerald's night camps no more than 5 miles apart. At this time Dempster confirmed that his guess of the week before was right, and that Fitzgerald and his men had been forced to return to McPherson. He concluded correctly that he was seeing camps made by the men of the Lost Patrol both on their trek out and on their retreat.

Two days later, Dempster's men arrived at the Mountain Creek cabin and found the toboggan, tarp and seven sets of dog harnesses Fitzgerald had cached there on his retreat. More significantly, they also discovered *"the paws of a dog cut off at the knee joint, also a shoulder blade which had been cooked and the flesh evidently eaten."*

Dempster reached the Caribou River on the cutoff on March 18. In striving to follow the trail of the Lost Patrol, he noted that the section of the country through which they were traveling was completely new to all of the men of his patrol. He commented: *"It has been up and down hill all afternoon. . . . Think the route we followed today much longer than going over the mountain."* Indications were that Fitzgerald's patrol had taken the long way in both directions on the cutoff. This may have been due to the fact that they were lost when they first met the party of Indians on the trip south, and had followed their packed, outward route on the retreat.

Dempster started down Trail River on the morning of March 19. That night he camped 5 miles from the Peel River. The next day, Dempster and his men mushed to Colin Vitisik's cabin, located on the Peel River about 8 miles below the mouth of Trail River. They were hanging up some of their gear to dry, when Dempster noticed a couple of packages on a roof beam. Charlie Stewart, Dempster's Indian guide, pulled them down to take a look, and discovered Fitzgerald's dispatch and mail bags. Despite the fact that Fitzgerald and his men had been virtually incapacitated by cold and starvation, they had persisted in toting at least 30 pounds of mail. Dempster also found a pile of dog bones in the cabin.

Considering the extremely poor condition the men of the Lost Patrol were in on February 5, it probably took them 2 days or until February 7 to reach Colin's cabin.

About 10 miles down from Colin's cabin, on Seven Mile Portage (which cuts off a bend in the Peel north of the cabin), Dempster found a tent, tent poles, a stove, a plate and a thermometer. Dempster reached the Peel River again at 2 p.m. on the 21st. He found an abandoned toboggan and two sets of dog harness out on the ice, several miles from the north end of the portage, 10 miles from the spot on the portage where the tent was found, or roughly 20 miles from the cabin. The corporal noticed that all of the rawhide ground lashing had been cut off the sled. He then saw a blue kerchief tied to a willow on the left bank of the river. Dempster climbed the bank and walked back through a fringe of willows, and came upon a small, open camp. Here he found the bodies of Kinney and Taylor—the two younger men. He also found a camp kettle half full of moose hide cut in small pieces. The hide had evidently been boiled for stew.

The Lost Patrol probably reached this point on the trail on February 10 or 11. If two dogs were still alive at this point, it seems likely that the men would have been able to travel the 20 miles from the cabin in at least 4 days. If Taylor and Kinney had had enough strength to cook something, it would indicate that they may have lived several days after reaching the point where their bodies were found. This would place the date of their deaths around February 12 or 13, and possibly later.

Dempster cut some brush and covered the men, then proceeded toward Fort McPherson. He concluded that Fitzgerald and Carter had pushed on in hopes of obtaining help for the others. He hoped that he might be in time to find Carter and Fitzgerald alive. Corporal Dempster camped that night alongside the river. Next day, March 22, he broke camp at 7:25 a.m., and about 10 miles farther down the Peel on the right limit, one of Dempster's men kicked up a pair of snowshoes. The trail veered toward the bank. Dempster's party climbed the bank and found the bodies of Fitzgerald and Carter. At this point, the dead men were only 25 miles from Fort McPherson. Fitzgerald and Carter may have died at about the same time as, or after, Kinney and Taylor since it probably took them 2 days to go 10 more miles, or they could even have died before, depending on the condition of the others. It would be safe to say they all died between February 12 and February 15.

The relief patrol covered the bodies with brush and rushed on to Fort McPherson, where they arrived that evening.

On March 23, Corporal Somers, accompanied by Special Constable Jimmie Husky and Peter Ross, set out upriver to retrieve the remains of the men of the Lost Patrol. Somers and his men used missionary C. E. Whittaker's team, Peter Ross's and that of John Firth of the Hudson's Bay Company, as the Mounties at Fort McPherson had lost, with one exception, their entire complement of dogs.*

The Somers party camped the first night 18 miles up the Peel River, and at 9:30 a.m. the next day arrived at the spot where the bodies of Inspector Fitzgerald and Special Constable Carter were located. Somers's report pieced together the final moments of the doomed party:

> Inspector Fitzgerald and Carter were lying on the top of the river bank of the right limit, and back a little in the timber; the distance being about 26 miles from Fort McPherson. I found the bodies covered with a half blanket also over each. The body of Constable Carter was lying about 10 feet from Inspector Fitzgerald, and had evidently been dragged and laid out immediately after death, as both hands had been crossed on the breast and the face covered with a handkerchief.
>
> Inspector Fitzgerald was lying where a fire had been, and was stiffened to the contour of the ground the right hand lying on the breast.

Somers did not make an extensive search of the clothes of the two men at the spot he found them, but a summary search revealed a piece of paper on which Fitzgerald had written his will with a bit of charred wood. It read: "All money in dispatch bag and bank, clothes, etc., I leave to my dearly beloved mother, Mrs. John Fitzgerald, Halifax. God bless all. F. J. Fitzgerald, R.N.W.M.P."

*The exception was one dog that had escaped from Fitzgerald's patrol at the very beginning of his journey, between Herschel Island and Fort McPherson. He was replaced by another dog at Fort McPherson. Later the runaway returned safely to Herschel Island.

Somers found his own watch in Carter's pocket, which he had given to Constable Taylor to have repaired in Dawson City. The Corporal picked up three snowshoes, all of which were broken, one camp kettle, one cup and one very blunt ax.

Somers placed the bodies of the two men on Peter Ross's sled, and Ross took them in, arriving at McPherson at 7 p.m.

While Ross mushed north down the Peel River, Somers and Husky went south another 10 miles and found the blue kerchief marking the camp of Kinney and Taylor. Constable Kinney was lying on his back with his hands crossed on his chest, indicating that he had no doubt died before Taylor, and Taylor had placed his hands in this position. Taylor, however, was found in a very crooked position, having shot himself with the .30-30 carbine. The gunshot had left him virtually unrecognizable. Whether Taylor committed suicide to avoid the temptations of cannibalism or to take himself out of his misery will never be known.

In lifting the men up to place them on the sled, Somers found a gunny sack containing Fitzgerald's diary as well as a small notebook that had belonged to Constable Kinney, a pocket barometer, some old socks, duffle coats and moccasins. These were found under the robe upon which Kinney and Taylor had been lying. Somers (and Dempster earlier) found two sleeping bags ("robes") covering the two men.* He also found around the camp a blunt ax and two camp kettles, one of which was lying behind Taylor's head and through which the bullet that killed him had traveled. A pocket watch and chain was found on Kinney's body.

At 4 p.m. on March 24, Somers and Husky placed the bodies on the sled and mushed downriver to where they had found Fitzgerald and Carter, and camped there for the night. It must have been a night that neither Somers nor Husky would ever forget.

One can visualize Corporal Somers and Jimmie Husky

*The Reverend C. E. Whittaker, in a letter to Bishop Stringer which is published with Mountie reports on the Lost Patrol, said that four sleeping robes were found with Kinney and Taylor. This is the only mention made of the fourth robe.

wrapped in their sleeping bags in front of the campfire, with Somers propped up on one elbow to see the diary better in the firelight. He begins to read the diary out loud, his breath visible as he speaks. The northern lights flicker overhead, and the wind moans through the snow-covered spruce trees. As Somers reads the tragic diary, he occasionally glances across the campfire at the bodies of his former comrades. It must have been quite a blow to Somers. Four friends—the entire complement of lawmen in the North with the exception of himself, Constable Blake at McPherson and Constable Wissenden at Herschel—were dead. Two others whom Somers had known were also gone. Sergeant Selig, who had been left on Herschel Island, had died of a throat ailment January 29, and former Special Constable Darrell had disappeared. Six deaths in less than 3 months would have been a tremendous psychological blow to men so dependent upon one another.

Somers and Husky arrived back at Fort McPherson in mid-morning on March 25. Dempster and Somers made a thorough search and examination of the remains of the men that afternoon.

The privations of the men of the Lost Patrol were incredibly harsh, judging by Somers's description. He reported that their hips and lower ribs showed prominently and their stomachs had fallen inward. He noted that Inspector Fitzgerald's toes were slightly frozen and very swollen. A thin skin was peeling off his fingers. Constable Kinney's feet had swollen to almost twice their normal size and the big toe of the right foot was badly peeled to the raw flesh. The condition in which Taylor and Carter were found was little better than the rest. Carter's toes were frozen and his hands bandaged. The flesh of all the men was of a reddish-black color, with a thin layer of skin peeling off. All their outer clothing was very badly torn and much scorched by fire, including socks, duffles, mitts and moccasins.

Corporal Somers hired three Natives to dig one large grave. The Reverend C. E. Whittaker, who had spent so much time with Fitzgerald on Herschel Island, supplied Somers with 250 feet of lumber and helped him make four coffins. A special service was held in the Church of England mission on Sunday, March 26. Nine white men and Mrs. Whittaker and a number of Loucheux Indians attended the service.

Two days later the funeral took place in the mission churchyard. The four men were buried with full military honors, including a salute fired by an honor guard of five men. The common grave was left open until Corporal Somers could obtain a copper kettle and cut out the name of each man and attach it to the coffin.

On March 30, Dempster set out for Dawson City with the shocking news of the death of the men of the patrol, as well as that of Sergeant S. E. A. Selig and of the disappearance of Darrell. Dempster discovered one additional camp made by the Lost Patrol which he had missed on his trip north. This camp was located about 5 miles north of Colin's cabin. Dempster made good time, and it took his patrol only 2 days to reach the cabin.

The weather was warm and clear for several days, then a gale blew in. But the men and dogs traveled well, and by April 5 were back on the Peel River; they had covered the approach to and traversed the entire Mountain Creek cutoff in 7 days. This was 5 days less than Fitzgerald had taken on his trip out.

Dempster and his men moved up the Peel into the Wind River and ascended that. The gale had covered much of their back trail, making the going difficult. One dog was bitten in a fight and had to be eased out of harness for a few days. Dempster and Turner suffered mild cases of snow blindness. One day the weather warmed up to a comparatively hot 17°F, making it too wet for efficient dog-sled travel. The heavy trail was hard going. River ice became even more treacherous than usual. Fyfe and Stewart both fell through the ice on two different occasions.

Five miles below Mount Deception, the men found the Wind River running completely open. They circled the open stretch and reached Forrest Creek on April 10. Here they met a party of Indians and followed a trail broken by them all the way across to Christmas Creek, which was only a few miles from the Indian Camp on the Blackstone River. They reached a cabin on the upper reaches of the Blackstone River on April 14. Two days later they reached the powerhouse on Twelve-mile River. Dempster tried to report his arrival by the telephone, but was unable to get through and proceeded to Twelvemile Roadhouse, arriving at 7 p.m. The call to Dawson was completed by the powerhouse staff during the night, and a fresh team met Dempster the next morning. He went ahead of the others and arrived at Dawson City at 10:30 a.m. on April 17. The others of the patrol arrived at 1:20 p.m.

The Dempster patrol made the fastest time of any Royal North-West Mounted Police patrol to that date, covering the 475-mile journey in just 19 days, averaging 25 miles a day.

The word was passed from Dawson City by telegraph the night of April 17, 1911. Newspapers throughout the world carried the story of the deaths of the four men of the patrol, Sergeant Selig at Herschel Island, and of Darrell's disappearance.

Fitzgerald's mother was the first one to hear authoritative news of the tragedy, through a dispatch sent to her in Halifax, Nova Scotia, by A. B. Perry, Commissioner of the Mounted Police at Regina. An early report in the Halifax newspapers suggested that Fitzgerald and his men had perished in a snow-slide. This was cleared up by Perry's dispatch.

The most ironic news of all was datelined Ottawa, April 18. It stated that the four men of the patrol had been selected to join a complement of Mounties scheduled to attend the coronation of King George V that summer.

Inspector Fitzgerald had completed 21 years of service and had 2 years to go on a 3-year reenlistment. At the end of 23 years of service, he would have been eligible to retire on a pension of $1,000 a year.

Speculation in respect to Fitzgerald's future is of some interest. World War I was to break out only 3 years after the tragedy. Fitzgerald would have had at least the rank of captain, at that time equivalent to the rank of inspector in the

Mounties. He had a surprising number of acquaintances in high places. With his combat experience in the Boer War, he could conceivably have earned rapid promotion, and, if he survived the slaughter long enough, it is not unrealistic to suppose that he might have achieved significant rank.

Chapter 10
Reflections

Numerous questions concerning the fate of the Lost Patrol have arisen through the years, and since no man was left alive to answer them, much is solely conjecture. The big question, of course, is *why* the tragedy happened.

Simply answered, the men died because they ran out of food and starved to the point where exhaustion, the cold and possibly scurvy killed them. They ran out of food because they spent too much time looking for the Forrest Creek trail. The ultimate responsibility for this decision (or lack of decision) has to rest squarely on the shoulders of Inspector Fitzgerald. Ostensibly, if he had kept better track of his supplies he would have turned back much sooner.

However, if the answer was that simple the tragedy never would have occurred. Various aspects of the disaster have to be looked at more closely before the reasons for it become clear and can be understood.

The author queried Major Frank Riddell, Canadian Corps of Signals, Retired, an expert on survival for the Canadian Army who spent over 40 years in the Arctic on a variety of assignments, as to the adequacy of the food value of the patrol's supplies. After scanning the list, Riddell pointed out that the supplies were lacking in nutritional value for the survival of the men.

"They were on a scurvy diet from the beginning," Riddell said. *"Even if the patrol had not gone anywhere, they would have been ill living on their limited supply of proteins and fats."*

A dietician for the government of Alaska, Winston Osborn, calculated the amount of calories per day for a 1-month trip (Fitzgerald had expected it would take about 30

116

days to reach Dawson City) for four men based on the list of supplies taken by the patrol. Osborn found the calorie supply to be 5,519 per man per day, of which 6% was protein, 14% fat, and 80% carbohydrates. Normal consumption at 68° to 77°F by today's standards calls for 2,800 calories, consisting of 9% protein, 41% fat, and 50% carbohydrates. Obviously, since fat should account for 41% of a normal diet at these warm temperatures, the 14% supply of the patrol, with temperatures as much as 135° lower, was woefully inadequate.

Fitzgerald probably had little choice in the matter of his food supplies. Supplies were hard to come by at a frontier post such as Fort McPherson. That was one of the governing factors in the Mounties' choice of Dawson City as the normal originating point for the patrol. Proper supplies were plentiful at that much-larger center, a Mountie Division Headquarters.

"It would appear from looking at their supplies that Fitzgerald almost certainly figured on shooting game along the way," Major Riddell observed. *"In fact, to get through without undue hardship, a lengthy patrol would have to depend on hunting, and food caches, or the prospect of purchasing meat and fish from the Indians."*

Riddell expressed some degree of surprise in noting that the patrol had only one firearm with them, a .30-30. *"An experienced arctic traveller will never go out on an extensive trip without a .22 rifle to complement a heavier caliber weapon,"* the Major said. *"A shotgun is another weapon of considerable utility in shooting rabbits, ptarmigan, or, if starving, birds. This oversight is incomprehensible in light of the length of the journey the Mounties had in front of them."*

117

Major Riddell pointed out that there were other implements useful in obtaining food which the patrol had not taken. *"I see no mention of snares. You certainly cannot reject snares because of their weight. Rabbits are caught by setting snares at night in their runways. The next morning when you get up, you have them for food. Of course, some years there are no rabbits because of that strange cycle of theirs. This may have been the case with the Lost Patrol,"* Riddell commented.

He said that another item of value in obtaining food was a gill net. This was usually carried by any party that planned to travel for an extensive period in the arctic bush.

The low nutritional value of supplies the patrol started with and the absence of vital firearms and other implements to obtain additional food along the way must have contributed significantly to the chain of events that led to the disaster.

"If Fitzgerald had hired an Indian guide to take him all the way through to Dawson City, he never would have missed the Forrest Creek trail," said Riddell, *"but it goes deeper than that. There is no hunter like an Indian hunter. He will find game—if there is any around—where none but the most skillful white man will be successful."*

Riddell was also concerned about the lack of a sufficient number of trailbreakers as a factor in the patrol's failure to find game. *"There are a number of reasons for having several trailbreakers,"* the major said. *"Two men can get up early in the morning and set out breaking trail far ahead of the dog teams. They are more likely to come across moose or caribou while doing this because the dogs aren't nearby yelping a warning. The men can swap off breaking trail and hunting. One man hunts while the other searches out the best trail. The combined weight of the two men sets up a well-packed trail for the dogs to follow. This takes a tremendous strain off the dogs. It is hard to figure why Fitzgerald attempted the trip with only four men and three teams, unless, of course, he could find no other men willing to go with him."*

If Hubert Darrell had not disappeared on the Anderson River and had made the trip to Dawson City as he had planned to do, Fitzgerald would have had the added trailbreaker so sorely needed, and would also have had a man who knew the way. (The regular police interpreter at McPherson, Jimmie Husky, had been asked to go but would not. Two other Natives had volunteered, but Inspector Fitzgerald declined their services.)

"A number of very common yet light food items which the patrol could have carried with them were rolled oats, rice and pemmican," Major Riddell said in commenting on the Mounties' nutritional problems. *"The food value of such items, particularly for cold country, is very high . . . It is difficult to understand why these foods were not in their provisions.*

"When they ran low on the Little Wind, if they had set snares at night for rabbits, or lynx, they would have helped their diet. An Indian guide would know where to look for moose. At that time of the year they usually gather up in river bottoms to feed on willow buds and patches of swamp grass.

"There are also porcupines which often can be found in spruce groves on the sunny side of creeks. They can be killed quite easily even if you don't have a .22. And of course, caribou are also common to that area, but you have to know where to hunt them."

To look at the breakdown of their supplies of bacon and flour after 27 days on the trail is to see how crucial the food problem was by the time Fitzgerald decided to turn back.* At this point, they had 8 pounds of bacon left and 10 pounds of flour, or a total of 11 ounces of bacon and 13 ounces of flour per man per day for 3 days. If the patrol had been 3 days out of Dawson City at this point—where it should have been— they would have completed the trip quite handily. As it was, under the best of circumstances the patrol was still 18 days away from either Dawson City or Fort McPherson. All they had left now was a starvation ration of fish and dog.

*Corporal Somers reported Fitzgerald estimated in the neighborhood of 30 days for the trip. This was about average, indicating the inspector did not expect to break any travel records. A projection like this did not offset the fact that most of the patrols did try to make better time than their predecessors.

119

A combination of factors probably caused Inspector Fitzgerald to disregard the serious consequences of his dwindling supplies. For one thing, he may have been mesmerized by his own seeming indestructibility. He had never failed to come through before. At crucial moments, fortune had always turned his way. This held true on the Moodie patrol in 1897, when the men ran out of food short of reaching Fort Grahame. Luckily, they reached the post the next day.

Good fortune again looked his way on several occasions during the 56-day journey from Dawson City to Fort McPherson during the winter of 1905-6. The Mapley patrol, of which Fitzgerald was a part, reached a crucial point in their food supply several times, but providentially either met Indians who sold them meat or were able to shoot moose or caribou to stretch out their staple food supply.

Another time, when Fitzgerald ran out of supplies on a whaleboat trip from Herschel Island to Fort McPherson, a Native who happened along gave the Mountie and his companions some fish. Since it was spring, they were not in a survival situation, but nevertheless, the offer of food saved the men an uncomfortable time.

Inspector Fitzgerald had also come through numerous engagements in the Boer War without a scratch.

It is not unusual for men of adventure to feel they are invulnerable to misfortune after surviving a number of crises. This may have caused Fitzgerald to press on, gambling his own life and the lives of his men in the expectation of finding additional food.

The crux of the tragedy was Carter's inability to find the trail. The assumption that Fitzgerald had been using the distances recorded by Mapley in 1904-5 is given credence by a statement made by Commissioner A. Bowen Perry in his official report of the tragedy. Perry noted that Fitzgerald had estimated the distance traveled up the Little Wind River as 55 miles. He then added: *"According to the table of distances submitted by Constable Mapley . . . the trail follows the Little Wind River for 54 miles, so that, assuming Inspector Fitzgerald's correct in his distances, he could not have been very far from Forrest Creek, up which he should have turned to cross the Wind-Hart divide."*

The fact that Commissioner Perry referred to Mapley's table in the way he did indicates that it was accepted as correct. But in reality, according to my own computations, the distance along the Little Wind River could not have been 54 miles as stated by Mapley, but was closer to 40—a difference of roughly 14 miles. Since Mapley's figures were very accurate everywhere else, what happened at the Little Wind River? Did the Mapley patrol come into the river at a point other than the Forrest Creek junction? Mapley's figuring may be the key to the cause of the disaster, and may explain the quandary in which Carter and Fitzgerald found themselves.

Looking at Mapley's report for his patrol of 1904-5, he says they ascended a short tributary of the Hart River (later called Waugh Creek) where a low divide *"is crossed to reach the Little Wind River."* There is no mention of a tributary of the Little Wind because the creek they followed, to Mapley, *was* the Little Wind River. Later this creek was named Forrest Creek. From the point where Forrest Creek is reached from the west to the big Wind River, it *is* 54 miles. Forrest Creek, or the part of it along which the trail ran, is about 13 or 14 miles long. From its intersection with the Little Wind River, the trail was 40 miles long to the big Wind.

In other words, going from west to east on the trail, Mapley considered the Forrest-Little Wind all one river, 54 miles in length. It is almost a straight run from west to east with no problems. However, going from east to west, if Forrest Creek is missed, the musher will suddenly find himself going almost due south, because the Little Wind has a sharp bend in it just past the junction with Forrest Creek. (See the map on page 97.)

The fact that Fitzgerald and his men were not looking for Forrest Creek until they had journeyed up the Little Wind 50 miles makes it a reasonable assumption that they were going by Mapley's table of distances, although it does not seem likely that they had the complete table with them. I conclude that Fitzgerald was going by only a word-of-mouth knowledge of the table and that this was confused and added incorrectly to other directions, including Carter's recollections. The result was that it never dawned on Carter or Fitzgerald that the 54 miles *included* Forrest Creek, and was not *to* Forrest Creek. Looking back at Commissioner Perry's statement, we see that the commissioner himself would have made the same mistake had he been with the patrol.

In fact Forrest Creek splays into four or five streamlets that enter the Little Wind. These are overgrown with willows and alders and failing to recognize the correct one would not be unusual for someone unfamiliar with the trail.

Maps were scarce items in those days, and the men of the patrol apparently had not had a satisfactory map available at the time they were looking for Forrest Creek, though they had been in possession of Hubert Darrell's sketch map when they started out. Corporal Somers, who had given the map to Fitzgerald, had declared it to be too small in scale to be of much use to anyone other than a man who had been over the trail (yet Carter *had* been over the trail). At any rate, the map failed them. Did Fitzgerald lose it before it was needed? Was it faulty or misinterpreted? Since both the user of the map and the map's originator died that winter and the map was not recovered, the answers remain hidden and leave the tantalizing question of why the men did not start looking for Forrest Creek until they were well past it.

The confusion over Forrest Creek did not end with the Fitzgerald tragedy. Map makers have consistently erred in locating Forrest Creek and the Little Wind River since the days of the Mountie patrols. On some maps Forrest Creek is shown as being part of the Little Wind River. On other maps Forrest Creek is shown to flow into the Little Wind from the north when it really comes in from the west. One map shows the creek to be considerably east of the mouth of the creek named by the Mounties, and it is misspelled "Forest" Creek. At the time of writing, the Department of Energy, Mines and Resources in Canada is investigating the problem and expects to make corrections when the next new editions of the relevant maps are published.

Fitzgerald had a compass, but there does not seem to have been any body of general or specific compass directions for the route in his or anyone else's hands. Possibly, after his fruitless search for the creek, Inspector Fitzgerald could have led the men on a course straight west in order to get into the Hart River drainage, but by this time he may have been reluctant to launch out even farther from the regular route. It must be remembered that the patrol had gotten off the trail (lost?) even before they had completed the Peel cutoff, and that both Fitzgerald and Carter had been over that section before. Following this, if Fitzgerald had been honest with himself, he should have either retained the Indian, Esau, to take him all the way through, or turned back.

The return trek to Fort McPherson was fraught with decisions for Inspector Fitzgerald, and the lives of the men depended on his reasoning. When the patrol fought its way back to the Mountain Creek cabin 4 miles from the south end of the cutoff, Fitzgerald must have considered staying there until game was shot, or wandering Indians drifted through the area, from whom he could have obtained help. His decision to continue rather than to remain at the cabin would probably have been based in part on the psychological advantages of maintaining some kind of activity as against remaining relatively immobile in a cabin. Inactivity leads to poor morale. Fitzgerald noted in his diary that at this point the dogs and men were very weak. Possibly he should have remained in the cabin for several days to rest and warm up, even though they were short of food.

Once again fate intervened in the form of mild weather. The next morning it warmed to -20°F, excellent for dog-sled travel. Fitzgerald would have had no reason to suppose that the warmer weather might not hold and the opportunity would have been too good to miss, so they took to the trail. They had mushed up Mountain Creek for only a few hours when the temperature plummeted to -51°F. During the next 6 days, the weather conditions offered little relief as the men struggled northward across the cutoff. No Indians came by to help. No moose or caribou wandered across the patrol's path

123

to provide food at the right moment. The fact that the four Mounties managed to win their way across the Mountain Creek portage—difficult even for men in good health—is testimony to their courage.

The Mounties had four dogs left when they reached the Peel, and Dempster was to find a pile of dog bones in Colin's cabin, 8 miles down the Peel River. Quite possibly, Fitzgerald took time to rest here in hopes that the men could gain enough strength for one last dash for Fort McPherson.

Of no little interest is the fact that Fitzgerald's diary was found underneath the sleeping robe used by Taylor and Kinney. Why was the diary there? Since Carter and Fitzgerald were apparently stronger than the younger men and journeyed on for another 10 miles before they died, one wonders why the inspector did not keep the diary with him. Fitzgerald might have feared that Carter would outlast him and destroy the record of Carter's failure to find the trail.

At this point, the record of the patrol may have meant more to Inspector Fitzgerald than life itself. A year later, Captain Robert Falcon Scott died on the trail with his companions in Antarctica after his epic journey to the South Pole. In his journal he displayed an almost macabre interest in what would be thought of him after he died. Scott was also quite proud of the fact that he, a man in his forties, had outlasted men in their twenties.

Oddly, Carter and Fitzgerald, both 41, lasted longer on the trail than Taylor and Kinney, who were in their twenties. Experts on survival say the reason for this is that the older men usually know how to pace themselves better than the younger. It is also apparent, from Dempster's and Somers's reports, that the older men left their sleeping bags with Taylor and Kinney. It was a gallant thing to do, especially in view of the fact that they had 35 more miles to go to Fort McPherson. Such an unselfish act on the part of the two men proved their courage, for they almost certainly invited their own deaths by leaving their sleeping bags with their younger companions.

The evidence is clear that Fitzgerald died after Carter. He had dragged Carter's body 10 feet from the fire, crossed the ex-Mountie's arms over his body and placed a handkerchief over his face. In Fitzgerald's condition it must have required a great effort to do this, which makes one wonder why he took the trouble.

Corporal Dempster attributed the failure of the patrol to a combination of factors—the small quantity of provisions taken, the want of an efficient guide, the delay in searching for the lost trail. But in the end, perhaps those were just symptoms; the real cause of the tragedy of the Lost Patrol may have been due to the fierce pride of its leader, Frank Fitzgerald. For him, a veteran of the Arctic, to find himself lost, unable to follow a well-established route of travel, would be difficult to accept. To have to return to Fort McPherson, with the prospect of informing his superiors that he could not find the way, would be a bitter blow. The decision to retreat would be taken with the greatest reluctance. This reluctance would have rendered his judgment and his timing faulty, and brought about the fatal consequences.

But despite this failure, Inspector Francis J. Fitzgerald remains a heroic pioneer of the North Country. His death, and the deaths of the men with him, after fighting for so long to survive under such terrible conditions, were to bring everlasting glory to the Mounted Police, and, in a sense, turned defeat into victory.

Epilogue

The Dawson City-Fort McPherson patrols continued to run until 1921. After that, deterioration of the whaling industry at Herschel Island and the establishment of radio communication ended the need for them. One final patrol was run from Herschel Island to Dawson City in 1945, the last ever made other than a commemorative patrol in 1970. In 1914, the Mounties established a post on the Porcupine River at Rampart House (old Rampart), and from there (and later from Old Crow), the patrols were made to Fort McPherson, Aklavik, Herschel Island and back to the Porcupine by a circular route. The tragedy of the Lost Patrol of 1910-11 was never repeated.

The shock of the tragedy led to effective measures to avoid a recurrence. Future patrols always hired Indian guides, minimizing the danger of losing the trail. The following December, Sergeant Dempster established a supply cache at a cabin built by John Martin at Christmas Creek, near the Blackstone, which was for the exclusive use of the Mounties during the time of year the patrol was being made. Later, another cabin was built on Trail River to provide a permanent store of food for the patrols, and still more caches were established along the route, to make doubly sure no patrol ran short of supplies.

Soon after Dempster returned from stocking John Martin's cabin, he set out again on the regular Fort McPherson patrol. Making the patrol with him were Constable F. W. Schutz, Special Constables A. Campbell, F. Turner and the Indian guide, Charles Stewart.

This patrol might well have been labeled the "Housekeeping Patrol," as one of the tasks the men accomplished along

126

the way was blazing the trail in areas where it might be missed. The Forrest Creek trail was blazed at the mouth of the creek by making what was called a "lobstick" or "lopstick" of two spruce trees. This was done by stripping the trees so that they were bare except for the top branches and two branches left to protrude lower down. Why the trail had not been marked during the years it had been in use before 1910 is a mystery. A few strokes of an ax applied to trees at the mouth of Forrest Creek would likely have saved four lives. However, nothing is certain in the wilderness. A tree blazed today might blow down in a storm tomorrow. A storm can hide a blaze under a cover of wet snow.

Dempster and his men also blazed a trail from the head of Mountain Creek to the Caribou River, and then from the headwaters of that stream to the upper reaches of the Trail River. In the process, even Dempster and his men lost their way. Dempster reported:

We turned off for Trail River over the divide at 10 a.m., following the same route as last year. We stopped for dinner at 11:40 a.m. and started again at 1 p.m. At 3 p.m. we reached a bald knoll and lost our direction. We were now on the slope facing Trail River, and it was getting dusky and hazy, making the outline of the hills very indistinct. Had to get somewhere to camp so travelled eastward. After losing about three-quarters of an hour looking for a cutting or something to indicate the right direction, we travelled east for about half an hour, and then turned towards the north, following a draw until we came to small timber where we camped at 4:30 p.m.

Dempster's patrol was still lost the next morning.

Took a view of the country in a.m. and tried to locate our direction, but it was too cloudy and indistinct, so we started at 8:30 a.m. travelling in a generally northeasterly direction, and finally at 11 a.m. dropped down over a bad hill into a stream running in a general northeast direction, but very crooked. After travelling down this stream for a couple of hours we found that we were on Trail River, but had got on to it much higher than we should have.

Farther down the creek he found a letter, tied to a stick, from Corporal Somers. It advised him that a cabin had not yet been built on Trail River, but that a cache was marked with a lobstick at the mouth of the creek.

Dempster reached Fort McPherson on February 3. While there, Somers told him about two patrols he had made in the spring and summer. The first one was by dog team with Louie Cardinal and Jimmie Husky to Herschel Island, to carry the news of the death of Fitzgerald and his men. (According to Somers's report, Eskimos, on hearing of the inspector's death said, *"Too bad. Inspector good man."*) The second patrol was by canoe to Caribou River with a man named "Indian Enoch" and an interpreter he called Johnny. During that patrol, Somers searched the area where the bodies of Fitzgerald and Carter had been found. He discovered only a table knife. Farther upriver, he searched the camp of Kinney and Taylor and found some knives, forks and a leather belt.

Dempster again led the Dawson City-Fort McPherson patrol in the winter of 1912-3. Accompanying Dempster were Corporal F. W. Schutz, Constable C. W. Philips, and Special Constables F. Turner and John Martin. During this trip the weather was good most of the way, and other than some troubles with dogs freezing their feet, the patrol was uneventful.

The patrol of 1913-4 was led by Corporal W.J. Hocking with John Martin as guide, and Charley Rivers, Andrew Kunnizzi and Jacob Njootli as mushers with four five-dog teams. Sergeant Dempster went with the patrol, but not this time as commander. He was moving north to a new assignment, to set up a station and customs house at Rampart on the Porcupine River.

That winter was comparatively mild. Trapping and hunting were good and many people were on the trail. It took the patrol 30 days to make the trip to Fort McPherson. That was good time, considering that the load they carried included over 70 pounds of newspapers and mail, 40 pounds of customs papers, and stationery for Dempter's new station.

Ironically, Corporal Hocking, who had never before commanded the patrol nor even been on it, made the fastest trip ever to date by a Mountie patrol between McPherson and Dawson City. Hocking, Rivers, Kunnizzi, Njootli and John Martin completed the journey in 17 days—a daily average of 28 miles for the 475-mile trip. The reasons for the improved time were undoubtedly the better cache system for supplying dog food, moderate temperatures and an increase in activity throughout the area, which made the trails easier to travel.

The patrol during the winter of 1914-5 was commanded on the first leg from Dawson City to McPherson by Sergeant W. G. Edgenton. Accompanying him were Constables C. R. Thornback, E. Ward and L. R. Wilson, and guides Alfred Bonnetplume and Peter Alexie. The Mounties by this time had inaugurated an intensive two-week training program for new men before they left Dawson City. Constable Thornback, who later wrote about his trip, said of the course: *"We learned how to handle our dogs, how to harness and drive them, unharness and care for them, prepare their food and feed them. Before the end of our training period, men and dogs were in top physical condition. We were under constant surveillance for any sign of inability or show of weakness that might endanger the lives of others of the patrol. So much depended on perfection."*

Thirty pounds of mail were taken to Fort McPherson for Herschel Island and other stations in the North. The trip was uneventful, except that three sleds went through overflow ice in shallow water on the Wind River, and later Thornback fell 10 feet into a crevasse. Neither incident resulted in injury.

Edgenton was to remain at Fort McPherson for duty in the Arctic. Sergeant S. G. Clay took over the patrol for the return trip, which took 17½ days.

The last patrol for which the Mounties retained an extensive record was in the winter of 1915-6. Corporal Ward, who was promoted after making the trip the previous year, commanded the patrol. Others making the trip were Constables N. V. King, J. R. Hutchinson and H. Oldham, and guides John Martin and Peter Alexie.

Following this patrol, possibly because of the war, the published reports were shortened, giving few details unless something unusual occurred. Dempster came back to lead the last four patrols. He had led more of the Dawson City-Fort McPherson patrols than any other white man, had set speed records going both ways (on the 1920 patrol he made the return trip to Dawson City spending only 14 days on the trail!) and is generally credited as the best trail man the Mounties had in that area. Dempster rose to the rank of inspector before he retired. He died in 1964.

The observations of the leaders of the patrols over the years were of considerable value to prospectors, as were the trails broken by the Mounties every winter. But even today, with the exception of a number of temporary camps, the vast land drained by the Peel and its tributaries—the Ogilvie, Blackstone, Hart, Wind, Bonnet Plume and Snake rivers—has fewer than a dozen permanent residents in an area of 30,000 square miles. This land is still the home of the moose and caribou, the wolf and the bear. Of humans, only the ghosts of the Mountie patrols and the Indians they once met inhabit this wild, immensely beautiful, yet harsh wilderness.

Appendix A

H. G. Mapley's 1905 table of distances traveled on each stream.

Dawson City to mouth of Twelvemile River . . . . 18 miles
Up Twelvemile River . . . . 64 miles
Across Seela Pass . . . . 14 miles
Down Blackstone River . . . . 14 miles
Across Blackstone-Hart divide . . . . 20 miles
Down Little Hart River (West Hart River) . . . . . . 45 miles
Down Hart River . . . . 5 miles
Up tributary of Hart River (Waugh Creek) . . . . . 21 miles
Across Hart-Wind divide . . . . 10 miles
Down Little Wind River . . . . 54 miles
Down Wind River . . . . 49 miles
Down Peel River . . . . 10 miles
Up Mountain Creek . . . . 16 miles
Portage . . . . 37 miles
Trail River . . . . 28 miles
Down Peel River to Fort McPherson . . . . 70 miles

Total . . . . **475 miles**

Appendix B

Equivalent Wind Chill Temperatures

	Calm	5	10	15	20	25	30	35	40	Winds above 40 have little additional effect.
Wind Speed (miles per hour)										
40	35	30	25	20	15	10	10	10		
35	30	20	15	10	10	5	5	0		**Little Danger**
30	25	15	10	5	0	0	-5	-5		
25	20	10	0	0	-5	-10	-10	-15		
20	15	5	-5	-10	-15	-20	-20	-20		
15	10	0	-10	-15	-20	-25	-30	-30		
10	5	-10	-20	-25	-30	-30	-35	-35		**Increasing Danger**
5	0	-15	-25	-30	-35	-40	-40	-45		(Flesh may freeze within 1 minute)
0	-5	-20	-30	-35	-45	-50	-50	-55		
-5	-10	-25	-40	-45	-50	-55	-60	-60		
-10	-15	-35	-45	-50	-60	-65	-65	-70		
-15	-20	-40	-50	-60	-65	-70	-75	-75		
-20	-25	-45	-60	-65	-75	-80	-80	-85		
-25	-30	-50	-65	-75	-80	-85	-90	-95		
-30	-35	-60	-70	-80	-90	-95	-100	-100		**Great Danger**
-35	-40	-65	-80	-85	-95	-100	-105	-110		(Flesh may freeze within 30 seconds)
-40	-45	-70	-85	-95	-105	-110	-115	-115		
-45	-50	-75	-90	-100	-110	-115	-120	-125		
-50	-55	-80	-100	-110	-120	-125	-130	-130		
-55	-65	-90	-105	-115	-125	-130	-135	-140		
-60	-70	-95	-110	-120	-135	-140	-145	-150		

Temperature (degrees Fahrenheit)

Appendix C

Letter from Winston Osborn, Chief Nutritionist,
Department of Health & Welfare, State of Alaska

Dear Mr. North:

Re the rations for 30 days for four men from Fort McPherson
to Dawson winter of 1911, the estimated amounts are
as follows—

   5,519 calories per man per day of which—
   6% was protein
   14% was fat
   80% was carbohydrates

At normal activity and temperatures of 68°-77° F present
standards suggest the following calories per man per day—

   2,800 calories per man per day of which—
   9% is protein
   41% is fat
   50% is carbohydrates

Note: Present day food tables may not reflect actual
composition of foods available in 1911.

Sincerely,

(*signed*)
Winston Osborn

Appendix D

Comments of Vilhjalmur Stefansson on the deaths of Inspector Fitzgerald and his party. Stefansson was camped at Coal Creek, about half a mile east of Horton River, which drains into the Arctic Ocean, when Dr. Anderson brought him the news.

Fitzgerald and two of his companions, Kinney and Carter, I knew personally. The news struck me like a blow. There were many aspects of it, but the most personal one was that the last conversation I had had with Fitzgerald was one in which he told me his thorough disapprobation of my methods of travel, and that if I tried to follow them I should surely come to grief. And here we were in comfort and in plenty listening to the story of his tragic death.

He had been a man of great courage, as were all of his companions; but they had failed through the essential weakness of their system of travel, which was to take with them all the food which they thought they could possibly need on the journey, without making any preparations for gathering more from the country when their stores should become exhausted. The result was in that case, as it has been in so many others, that when unlooked-for circumstances stretched the time of the journey beyond the limit reckoned on at first, supplies ran out; the dogs were eaten, then the men's skin clothing and the harness of the dogs; and then came death through cold and starvation.

It is always easy to see when a tragedy has happened how it could have been avoided, but it has always seemed to me that so long as you are travelling in a country supplied with game, you are safer to start with a rifle and resolution to find food (but without a pound of food on your sled), than you would be in starting with a sled heavily loaded with food and with no provision made for getting more when the sled load has been eaten up.

Bibliography

PERSONAL INTERVIEWS—MEN WHO MADE THE
DAWSON CITY-FORT McPHERSON PATROL:
Richard Martin, Dawson City, Yukon Territory
Andrew Kunnizzi, Fort McPherson, Northwest Territories
Charles Rivers, Dawson City, Yukon Territory
Charles Thornback, San Juan Capistrano, California

BOOKS:
Berton, Pierre. *The Mysterious North.* New York: Alfred A.
   Knopf, 1956.
Bodfish, Hartson. *Chasing the Bowhead Whale.* Cambridge:
   Harvard University Press, 1936.
Camsell, Charles. *Son of the North.* Toronto: Ryerson, 1954.
Featherstonhaugh, R. C. *The Royal Canadian Mounted
   Police.* New York: Garden City Publishing Company,
   1940.
Mitchell, George. *The Golden Grindstone.* London: Chatto
   and Windus, 1936.
Stefansson, Vilhjalmur. *My Life with the Eskimo.* 1913.
   Reprint. New York: Collier Books, 1962.

RCMP REPORTS IN CANADA, SESSIONAL PAPERS:
Edmonton to the Klondike
Instructions to, and diary of, Inspector J. D. Moodie in
   charge of patrol from Edmonton to the Yukon 1897.
   Sessional Paper No. 15, Part II, 62 Victoria, A. 1898.
Dawson City to Fort McPherson
Constable H. G. Mapley, March 10, 1905. Sessional Paper
   No. 28, Part III, Appendix E, 5-6 Edward VII, A. 1906.
Constable H. G. Mapley, April 5, 1906. Sessional Paper
   No. 28, Part III, Appendix E, 6-7 Edward VII, A. 1907.
Constable A. E. Forrest, February 22, 1907. Sessional Paper
   No. 28, Part III, Appendix D, 7-8 Edward VII, A. 1908.
Constable W.J.D. Dempster, March 24, 1908. Sessional
   Paper No. 28, Part III, Appendix E, 8-9 Edward VII, A.
   1909.

Constable W.J.D. Dempster, March 17, 1909. Sessional Paper No. 28, Part III, Appendix C, 9-10 Edward VII, A. 1910.

Constable W.J.D. Dempster, March 17, 1910. Sessional Paper No. 28, Appendix D, 1 George V, A. 1911.

Special report—Includes reports, correspondence, etc., concerning the death of the late Inspector F. J. Fitzgerald and party on the McPherson-Dawson Patrol, 1910-11. Sessional Paper No. 28, Part V, 2 George V, A. 1912.

Sergeant W.J.D. Dempster, March 12, 1912. Sessional Paper No. 28, Part III, Appendix D, 3 George V, A. 1913.

Sergeant W.J.D. Dempster, March 22, 1913. Sessional Paper No. 28, Part III, Appendix C, 4 George V, A. 1914.

Corporal W. J. Hocking, March 6, 1914. Sessional Paper No. 28, Part III, Appendix C, 5 George V, A. 1915.

Sergeant W. G. Edgenton, February 3, 1915. Sessional Paper No. 28, Part III, Appendix D, 6 George V, A. 1916.

Sergeant S. G. Clay, March 5, 1915. Sessional Paper No. 28, Part III, Appendix E, 6 George V, A. 1916.

Corporal E. Ward, March 13, 1916. Sessional Paper No. 28, Part III, Appendix E, 7 George V, A. 1917.

Herschel Island

Inspector D. M. Howard, August 14, 1905. Sessional Paper No. 28, Appendix L, 5-6 Edward VII, A. 1906.

Inspector D. M. Howard, August 14, 1905. Sessional Paper No. 28a, Supplementary Report, Appendix A, 5-6 Edward VII, A. 1906.

Inspector D. M. Howard, August 1906. Sessional Paper No. 28, Appendix O, 6-7 Edward VII, A. 1907.

Inspector D. M. Howard, July 16, 1907. Sessional Paper No. 28, Appendix K, 7-8 Edward VII, A. 1907-8.

Inspector A. M. Jarvis, November 20, 1907. Sessional Paper No. 28, Appendix K, 8-9 Edward VII, A. 1909.

Staff Sergeant F. J. Fitzgerald, March 28, 1909. Sessional Paper No. 28, Appendix P, 9-10 Edward VII, A. 1910.

Staff Sergeant F. J. Fitzgerald, May 16, 1909. Sessional Paper No. 28, Appendix K, 9-10 Edward VII, A. 1910.

Staff Sergeant F. J. Fitzgerald, July 6, 1909. Sessional Paper

No. 28, Appendix Q, 9-10 Edward VII, A. 1910.

Sergeant S.E.A. Selig, April 1909. Sessional Paper No. 28, Appendix R, 9-10 Edward VII, A. 1910.

Sergeant S.E.A. Selig, June 30, 1909. Sessional Paper No. 28, Appendix L, 9-10 Edward VII, A. 1910.

Corporal J. Somers, May 3, 1911. Sessional Paper No. 28, Appendix S, 2 George V, A. 1912.

Other Patrols

Corporal J. Somers, Fort McPherson to Caribou Creek and return, June 7, 1911. Sessional Paper No. 28, Appendix T, 2 George V, A. 1912.

Sergeant W.J.D. Dempster, Dawson to Hart River and return with emergency supplies, December 22, 1911. Sessional Paper No. 28, Part III, Appendix C, 3 George V, A. 1913.

Superintendent C. Constantine, Trip to Mackenzie River with report of Sergeant Fitzgerald, Herschel Island Detachment, Fort Saskatchewan, September 6, 1902. Sessional Paper No. 28, Appendix D, 3-4 Edward VII, A. 1904.

NEWSPAPERS AND PERIODICALS:

Thornback, Charles R. "North Patrol." *Alaska magazine*, January 1972, p. 11; February 1972, p. 9.

Halifax Herald, April 18 and 19, 1911.

Halifax Morning Chronicle, April 18 and 19, 1911.

SPECIAL PUBLICATIONS:

Lathrop, Theodore G. *Hypothermia.* Portland: Mazama, 1973.

Washburn, Bradford. *Frostbite.* Boston: Museum of Science.

Adventure in the Northland comes fast and furious. You'll find more sure-fire reading excitement in these Alaska Northwest Publishing books:

TWO IN THE FAR NORTH — *A northern classic about a couple who explored the North's wildest places by poling boat, dog team, and on foot.*

THE NORWEGIAN: — *A Rollicking Tale of Wild Trails and the Lure of Gold.*

FRANK BARR — *Fly with the legend who always "fixed 'em up and flew 'em out."*

ALASKA BEAR TALES — *Spine-chilling accounts of actual bear attacks.*

THE LONG DARK — *A fascinating novel of survival in the Alaskan Bush.*

TRAILS OF AN ALASKA TRAPPER — *the personal story of a man's passion for living and working in the rugged North.*

This is just a partial list. Write us for a free catalog describing the whole Alaska Northwest Publishing library.

Alaska Northwest Publishing Company
130 Second Avenue South, Edmonds, Washington 98020
(206) 774-4111